TEACHINGS
— *for an* —
UNBELIEVING
WORLD

"What a joy to read this newly discovered series of reflections on the famous passage in Acts where Paul speaks to the skeptical Greeks about the 'unknown God.' Each brief teaching is a gem, taking us ever-deeper into the mind of St. John Paul II and the mystery of salvation."

Mary Ann Glendon
Learned Hand Professor of Law at Harvard University
Former US ambassador to the Holy See

"Here, then, is the antidote to modernity's tendency to dumb down the human person."

From the foreword by **George Weigel**
Distinguished Senior Fellow and
William E. Simon Chair in Catholic Studies
Ethics and Public Policy Center

"This book is one of the great hidden treasures unearthed in our time."

From the introduction by **Scott Hahn**
Founder of the St. Paul Center for Biblical Theology

TEACHINGS
— *for an* —
UNBELIEVING WORLD

Newly Discovered Reflections on
PAUL'S SERMON AT THE AREOPAGUS

JOHN PAUL II
ARCHBISHOP KAROL WOJTYŁA

Foreword by George Weigel
Introduction by Scott Hahn
Curator's Notes by Marta Burghardt

AVE MARIA PRESS AVE Notre Dame, Indiana

Foreword © 2019 by George Weigel

Introduction © 2019 by Scott Hahn

Curator's Notes (Afterword) © by Wydawnictwo Literackie, Kraków, 2018

First publication by Wydawnictwo Literackie, Kraków, 2018

English translation © 2019 Ave Maria Press, Inc. provided by IdeaHouse

Frontispiece of Bishop Karol Wojtyła © Catholic Press Photo

Founded in 1865, Ave Maria Press is a ministry of the United States Province of Holy Cross.

www.avemariapress.com

Hardcover: ISBN-13 978-1-59471-985-1

E-book: ISBN-13 978-1-59471-986-8

Cover image © AP Photo/Gianni Foggi

The original handwritten manuscript is part of the collection of the Kraków Metropolitan Curial Archives. The photographic image of it is used with the permission of Cardinal Stanistaw Dziwisz, Archbishop Emeritus of Kraków.

Cover and text design by Samantha Watson.

Printed and bound in Canada.

Library of Congress Cataloging-in-Publication Data
Names: John Paul II, Pope, 1920-2005, author.
Title: Teachings for an unbelieving world : newly discovered reflections on Paul's sermon at the Areopagus / Pope John Paul, II, Karol Wojtyla.
Other titles: Kazanie na Areopagu. English
Description: Notre Dame, Indiana : Ave Maria Press, 2020. | "First publication by Wydawnictwo Literackie, Kraków, 2018." | Summary: "In this newly discovered work, Karol Wojtyla uses St. Paul's sermon to the people of Athens in Acts 17 as a framework for articulating the faith in a culture of skepticism and unbelief. These thirteen brief homilies provide a compelling teaching for Catholics in today's post-Christian world and give fresh insight into John Paul II's pontificate"-- Provided by publisher.
Identifiers: LCCN 2019048659 (print) | LCCN 2019048660 (ebook) | ISBN 9781594719851 (hardcover) | ISBN 9781594719868 (ebook)
Subjects: LCSH: Bible. Acts, XVII, 17-24--Sermons.
Classification: LCC BS2625.54 .J64 2020 (print) | LCC BS2625.54 (ebook) | DDC 226.6/06--dc23
LC record available at https://lccn.loc.gov/2019048659
LC ebook record available at https://lccn.loc.gov/2019048660

CONTENTS

FOREWORD

BY GEORGE WEIGEL

That St. Paul's address to the Athenians on the Areopagus held a special place in the religious and pastoral imagination of St. John Paul II was vividly illustrated by the determination he showed in gently but firmly insisting that the "Mars Hill" of the ancient world be part of his itinerary when he visited Athens in May 2001, completing his Jubilee pilgrimage through the sites of salvation history. There had been considerable local opposition to holding an ecumenical meeting there, with various Greek Orthodox voices complaining of "Wojtyła's hegemonic tours." But John Paul was never one to let irrational bigotry get in the way of evangelical witness, so the Holy Synod of Greek Orthodoxy was finally persuaded to meet the pope where St. Paul had met the Athenian *bien-pensants* of his day, shortly after John Paul arrived in Athens on May 4, 2001. And after weeks of controversy over the very possibility of their meeting, the Orthodox clergy spontaneously applauded the bishop of Rome.

What did "the Areopagus" mean to John Paul II? I think it seemed to him a biblical metaphor for the Church's situation in post-Christian Europe, and indeed throughout the post-modern West: as the Apostle of the Gentiles had tried to introduce the Athenians to the "unknown God"—the one, true God—through language and imagery that began with the Athenians' own experience, so the Church of the twenty-first century and the third millennium must meet men and women where the Church finds them, in all their confusions and strivings, working from the material at hand (what we sometimes call *semina verbi*) to open cold hearts and brittle minds to the warmth and liberating truth of the Gospel.

It was a challenging image, of course, because St. Paul's initial efforts on the Areopagus met with resistance and little immediate success. But that, too, may have been part of the metaphor's attraction for Wojtyła, whose deep insight into the future may have included the intuition that great time and effort would be necessary to re-convert a post-Christian West to Christ, at least until things became so difficult that the men and women of the future would be willing to consider an alternative to the worship of the imperial autonomous Self. That phase of the twenty-first-century Catholic story remains to be told. But it must be said that the reaction of many Athenians to St. Paul was strikingly parallel to the reception John Paul II received among the *bien-pensants* of western Europe, including those who maintained some formal (and even hierarchical) affiliation with the Church. The inculturation of the Gospel in self-satisfied societies and cultures is never easy.

These Athenian meditations are also important because they preview several crucial themes that Karol Wojtyła would develop in his extensive papal magisterium over more than twenty-six years. These themes occur in small fragments throughout the text, but their brevity often enhances their clarity. Among the most important of these themes, I would note the following:

The Origins of the West. At the outset of his Athenian catecheses, Wojtyła asserts, as he would throughout his pontificate, that the deepest taproots of the civilizational project we call "the West" are to be found in Jerusalem and Athens—and, ultimately, in their interaction. Paul, the scholar-Pharisee who was obviously fluent in some currents of Greek philosophy, was the first to try to build a conceptual bridge between the two. After some centuries of hard intellectual work, that bridge was built and across it walked those who gave the Church the Nicene Creed and the dogmatic definitions of ecumenical councils such as Ephesus, Chalcedon, and Constantinople III. Jerusalem-and-Athens was not only crucial for the Church, however—it was central to shaping Western civilization.

What did "Jerusalem" teach the West? It taught the West that history is neither cyclical nor random, but linear and purposeful. History is going somewhere; so is humanity; and the foundational image for that sense of purposefulness and direction in Western civilization is the Exodus of Israel from bondage in Egypt. "Athens," for its part, taught the West that there are truths built into the world and into us; that we can know those truths with a measure of certainty through the arts of reason; and that knowing those truths, we come to understand our moral obligations, and what makes for human flourishing.

Wojtyła was acutely aware that the interaction of "Jerusalem" and "Athens" was essential to the development of Christianity's intellectual architecture, for "Athens" had given the Church born in and from "Jerusalem" the conceptual tools to turn kerygma ("Jesus is Lord") into creed and doctrine. And over the centuries, "Athens"—the arts of reason—had often helped purify Christianity from both heresy and superstition. By the same token, and as Paul's experience on the Areopagus vividly illustrated, "Jerusalem" challenged, and continues to challenge, "Athens" to raise its sights, to stretch its imagination, and to hear what the late Peter Berger called "signals of transcendence" in the world it analyzed through reason.

All that began, in some sense, with the Pauline experience on the Areopagus. Little wonder, then, that a philosopher-pope with a deep appreciation of Judaism, the pope who wrote that "faith and reason are like two wings on which the human spirit rises to the contemplation of the truth" (*Fides et Ratio*, 1), would be determined to make a pilgrimage there.

Humanity is theotropic. Throughout his pontificate, John Paul II lifted up a theme sketched in preliminary form in these catecheses: the human spirit has an innate yearning for the divine and a hardwired instinct for worship, such that, if true objects of belief and worship are not found, false objects of belief and worship will be. As he wrote in several of the earliest of these meditations, human beings thirst for answers to the great questions of life, including the question of why there is anything at all, the question of what purpose life has, and the question of what destiny awaits each of us. Those are philosophical questions, to be sure, and in *Fides et Ratio*, John Paul II challenged philosophy to recover its nerve, stop frittering away its energies on thinking-about-thinking-about-things, and take up the Big Questions again.

For Wojtyła, however, the Big Questions were also profoundly religious questions. The search for answers to them can lead to false gods, or the true God: but it will lead somewhere. He knew this in his bones. In the agony of the twentieth century, from his experiences under Nazism and communism, John Paul II saw the existential results of the worship of false gods. Like St. Paul, he wanted to turn humanity's innate religious instinct toward the true God who is alone worthy of worship—the God who, being worshipped, enlarges, rather than diminishes, worshipping humanity.

God is not an over-against. John Paul II's interest in phenomenology as a philosophical method is well known, but his philosophical work was grounded in an Aristotelian-Thomistic realism that confirmed what "Athens" had taught the West: there is something properly called *the* truth and we can know it. The Thomistic dimension of this philosophical foundation is apparent in the third of these meditations, where Wojtyła reminds us that the God of the Bible is not some super-Being in competition with the beings of this world (the mistake constantly made by the New Atheists). Rather, God is sheer Being itself—the God who identified himself to Moses and Israel as "I AM WHO I AM" (Ex 3:14) is the philosophers' *ipsum esse subsistens* (as Aquinas put it in *Summa Theologiae* 1:4.2), that-which-makes-all-other-being possible. And because this God is not in competition with "other beings," we can know God as "the inner mystery of every creature" and especially of the human person: the one, as St. Paul put it, in whom "we live and move and have our being."

Here, then, is the antidote to modernity's tendency to dumb down the human person. On the Areopagus, Paul subtly challenged the Athenians to think of themselves as grander than they had previously imagined: that was the lifting-up made possible by an encounter with the "unknown God," who is in fact the God who makes himself known in history, and comes into history to lead humanity to its true destiny. That Pauline theme would be at the center of John Paul II's papal magisterium for over a quarter century.

"Choice" is not everything. Athenians, or at least that minority of Athenians who were freemen, prided themselves on their freedom to choose, to be self-governing. That pride has been massively amplified in the contemporary world, where "choice" has become the word that stops all argument and willfulness is too frequently taken to be the index of maturity. In his fourth Athenian catechesis, Wojtyła briefly limned a theme that would become prominent in the second half of his pontificate, especially in the encyclicals *Centesimus Annus* and *Veritatis Splendor*: that the will must be related to the true and the good if our choosing is to be truly human. Sheer willfulness is childish; a mature freedom is one that seeks the truth freely, adheres to it freely because it leads us to the good, and does so out of moral habit. Freedom and responsibility, Wojtyła insists in this catechesis, are intimately linked, and a truly responsible, mature exercise of the will is one that is tethered to truth and ordered to goodness. This, he would insist in *Centesimus Annus*, is not just critical for individuals and their personal moral lives; it is just as important for the free and virtuous society.

Jesus Christ is the answer to the question that is every human life. In his Mars Hill catecheses, and particularly in his meditations on the meaning of the Incarnation, the Resurrection, and redemption, Wojtyła anticipates the radical Christocentricity that would characterize his papal magisterium. It was Paul's proclamation of the Resurrection of Jesus, of course, that quickly became a sign of contradiction to many of his Athenian listeners, some of whom could imagine the immortality of the soul but none of whom could grasp what a resurrected body could possibly be, or mean. Yet Paul insists, and Wojtyła underscores, that the Resurrection is the key, the sine qua non, to the entire Christian experience and proposal. No Resurrection, no encounter with the Risen One, no Christianity. Period. Conversely, meeting the Risen Lord, personally as St. Paul did, or in the act of faith and in the sacraments, changes everything—especially how we think about human destiny,

which is not just the avoidance of oblivion in some dis-
embodied state, but the glorification of what now is, in a
new state of being that is radically different but manifestly
human.

The most concise expression of this Easter faith artic-
ulated by the Second Vatican Council comes in paragraph
22 of *Gaudium et Spes*, the Pastoral Constitution on the
Church in the Modern World. There, the Council Fathers
wrote a powerful testament to Christian humanism (in
words I have long thought were likely crafted by the archbishop of Kraków, Karol Wojtyła): "Only in the mystery of
the Word made flesh does the mystery of man take on light.
. . . Christ the final Adam, by the revelation of the mystery
of the Father and His love, fully reveals man to man himself and makes his supreme calling clear." As Christ, the
incarnate Son of God and Risen Lord, reveals the face of the
merciful Father, he simultaneously reveals us to us. That was
what Paul was trying to get the Athenians to understand.
Convinced that a "pulverization" of the human person was
at the root of late modernity's crisis of crises, that is what
Karol Wojtyła proposed in his eighth Athenian catechesis—
and then throughout his pontificate.

Salvation is, at bottom, a matter of love. Like Paul,
Wojtyła in his seventh catechesis teaches that the "unknown
God," who has become known to Israel and is definitively
encountered in Jesus the Christ, wishes to save that which
he has created, which means redeeming the world from its
incompleteness and folly. That redemption requires judgment, for there is much that must be set aright. Yet in the

God Paul proclaimed, Wojtyła asserts, justice is reconciled with love, the "supreme witness" of which is the unbreakable bond between the Cross and the Resurrection. Raising his obedient, suffering servant Jesus from the dead to a new and supercharged realm of life, the God whom Paul had tried to introduce to Athens demonstrated that divine love is the most powerful thing imaginable, for it is more powerful than death itself.

The God whom Paul proclaims is thus more than an Unmoved Mover, a First Cause, even more than a Creator. The God of St. Paul is the Redeemer, "the One who has overcome everything," as Wojtyła puts it, because this God is love itself. The Yugoslav dissident Marxist Milovan Djilas once said that John Paul II was the only man he had ever met who was entirely without fear. The root of that fearlessness was John Paul II's unshakable conviction about the redemptive power of divine love—the same conviction that motivated St. Paul to undertake the mission *ad gentes*, and ultimately to die for it.

Love is self-gift. In the magisterium of John Paul II, citations of *Gaudium et Spes* 22 are frequently paired with citations of *Gaudium et Spes* 24 (another section of the Pastoral Constitution on the Church in the Modern World in which Wojtyła likely had an authorial hand): "Man cannot fully find himself except through a sincere gift of himself." Jesus Christ reveals the truth about us, we are taught in *Gaudium et Spes* 22. According to *Gaudium et Spes* 24, an essential part of that truth, demonstrated by Christ's Passion, Death, and Resurrection, is that self-gift, not self-assertion, is the royal road to human flourishing and ultimately to beatitude.

This is, obviously, a countercultural claim in the twenty-first-century West. Yet Wojtyła argued, as a philosopher, that while self-gift is at the center of an Easter-based Christian ethics, what he called the "Law of the Gift" could also be discovered in a disciplined reflection on the structure of human moral agency. Thus, once again, faith and reason, Jerusalem and Athens, can work together in a Pauline synthesis to lift the human spirit and raise human aspirations beyond the quest for immediate gratification and satisfaction.

Vatican II and the "New Evangelization." Wojtyła's catecheses quote extensively from the documents of the Second Vatican Council, and in this respect these meditations anticipate the extensive commentary on the council's texts that he would later prepare for the Synod of Kraków (published in English as *Sources of Renewal*). What, though, was the intention that underlay those conciliar texts and that binds them into a coherent whole?

Vatican II was many things to Karol Wojtyła. It was a second graduate-level education in theology, an encounter with thinkers and themes he had not previously met in his studies in Kraków and pre-conciliar Rome and his teaching at Lublin. It was a bracing, energizing first experience of the new Christians of the Third World; the spontaneity and clarity of the faith of the African bishops he met at the council left a deep impression on Wojtyła, and senior African churchmen, often first- or second-generation Christians, would play prominent roles in the pontificate of John Paul II. Perhaps above all, however, Wojtyła experienced Vatican II as what Pope John XXIII had intended his council to be: a new experience of Pentecost, from which the Church would enter its third millennium with revitalized evangelical zeal and a new passion for mission.

Vatican II, in other words, was intended to prepare the Church to be a community of disciples in mission: a community whose raison d'être was to offer others the gift it had been given—friendship with the Lord Jesus Christ and incorporation into the communion of his friends, the Church.

Little wonder, then, that Karol Wojtyła, who lived Vatican II as a Pentecostal experience summoning the Church to mission, should be fascinated by St. Paul and the Areopagus. And as pope, Wojtyła would put evangelism at the very center of his teaching, using the image of the Areopagus in the encyclical *Redemptoris Missio (The Mission of the Redeemer)* to illustrate the sectors of late-modern and post-modern society where the laity were particularly fit to be the agents of evangelization: the worlds of science and the media, the environmental and women's movements, the worlds of politics, culture, and economics. All of these Mars Hills awaited disciples willing to propose the true God as the answer to the twenty-first century's confusions about unknown gods or false gods. And it was John Paul II's purpose to call everyone in the Church to be a missionary disciple.

In *Novo Millennio Ineunte* (*Entering the New Millennium*), his apostolic letter closing the Great Jubilee of 2000, John Paul II adopted an image from the fifth chapter of Luke's gospel and summoned the Church to "put out into the deep" (Lk 5:5) of the late-modern and post-modern worlds—to leave the shallow, brackish waters of institutional maintenance and set out on the roiling, turbulent waters of the twenty-first century, in order to make a great catch: not of fish, but of souls.

Early echoes of that evangelical imperative can be found throughout Wojtyła's Athenian catecheses. Thus these meditations provide something of a preview of the great evangelical thrust of the pontificate of St. John Paul II, even as they underscore how his analysis of the contemporary human situation, and his understanding of how the Church must preach the Gospel under those circumstances, was remarkably consistent over four decades.

INTRODUCTION

BY SCOTT HAHN

In its Golden Age—the fifth century before Christ—Athens had everything a city might boast about: military might, intellectual firepower, artistic genius, architectural splendor, and stable government.

As ages go, though, it was brief. In the century that followed, the city was surpassed by Macedon, whose kings, first Philip and then his son Alexander, built an empire that reached all the way to India.

Yet the name of Athens retained a certain luster, a memory of greatness. Philosophers invoked it with reverence, and so did playwrights and historians. It was the city of Plato and Aristotle, Aeschylus and Sophocles, Herodotus and Thucydides. This influence continued long after Athens itself lay in ruins. America's founders, for example, looked to that ancient Greek city-state as the birthplace of democracy. They were not alone, as Athenian innovation was not confined to the political sphere, but was visible in diverse modes of intellectual and artistic expression, countless paths of inquiry.

By the time Paul set foot on the Areopagus, the city was largely a museum for the glorification of its singular past. The world's Roman overlords had given Athens special status and endowed its schools to preserve and promote their cultural heritage. (The legend went abroad that in one Athenian neighborhood, the children spoke before they were a month old.)

Paul was keenly aware of the symbolic importance of Athens—and his preaching there has taken on a corresponding importance in the story we tell about his ministry. How we understand that moment is crucial to our understanding of evangelization in any age.

Thus we can only be grateful to hold a book such as this in our hands—a sustained reflection on that moment, set to paper by an interpreter who was a genius and a saint—and would one day be a beloved pope. This book is one of the great hidden treasures unearthed in our time.

A proper consideration of St. John Paul II's interpretation, however, requires at least a glancing awareness of the original context of St. Paul's address. So let us turn our attention again to Athens and to antiquity.

In the Greek cities of Ephesus, Thessalonica, and Berea, Paul began his work in the synagogues of the Jews. There he could count on the shared heritage of Israel's ancient covenant with God.

In Athens too, we're told, he started in the synagogue, but he moved to the market, where he caught the attention of the intellectuals. They found Paul interesting—perhaps exotic or entertaining—and judged him worthy of an open hearing at the Areopagus, the city's thriving center of judicial activity and scholarly debate.

That was where Paul wanted to be. He longed to reach the minds of the men on that outcropping of rock, the men whose influence shaped the intellectual culture of the entire empire. To do so, he had to speak in a way that was different from his preaching to fellow Jews. At the Areopagus he could not count on the common language and history of Israel. It would be absurd to cite the Law or the Prophets to people who did not recognize their authority. So Paul drew first from the culture of the Athenians.

Scholars will sometimes treat the apostle's preaching in Athens as opportunistic and almost random. But I maintain that his rhetorical choices were deliberate and artful; they are instructive for those of us who often find ourselves addressing unbelievers—men and women of good will who do not share our assumptions, goals, or religious vocabulary.

Paul trains his attention on two cultural artifacts: an altar and a poem. A *particular* altar and a *particular* poem. Again, his choices do not appear to be random or merely convenient.

Behind both artifacts stands one remarkable, semi-historical, semi-mythical figure. His name is Epimenides. He lived on the island of Crete in the sixth or seventh century before Christ. Epimenides was a shepherd who one day, according to legend, fell asleep in a cave and awoke fifty-seven years later. He emerged from the cave transfigured, filled with divine gifts. Before, he had been a tender of sheep; now he was a prophet, a vatic poet, an inspired lawgiver, and a priest with singular expertise in sacrificial matters. He won renown on his native island, and his fame spread even to the Greek mainland, to the city of Athens, some 214 miles away.

Indeed, the Athenians sent a delegation to call upon him, because the city was in dire peril. One of its leading families, the Alcmaeonidae, had violated the sanctuary of a temple, committing murder at the altar in the aftermath of an uprising. Afterward the city was riven by political strife, stricken by pestilence, and visited by strange, unexplainable phenomena. There was general agreement that the Alcmaeonidae had brought a curse upon the city, and the citizens were helpless to overcome it.

The story is preserved in testimonies from leading Greeks of the generations that followed: Plato, Aristotle, Plutarch, Diogenes Laertius, Pausanias, Strabo, and others. The episode is treated almost as a refounding of Athens.

When Epimenides arrived in the city, he suggested that perhaps there was a god yet unknown to them, who would be willing and able to help Athens if the appropriate sacrifices were offered. He asked his hosts to bring a number of sheep, some black and some white, to the Areopagus. The prophet then allowed the sheep to roam and graze where they pleased. Wherever a sheep lay down, it was sacrificed to "the god." (Plato, in his telling of the story, uses the definite article: *ho theos*.) In each of those places, an altar was built. Almost a millennium later, Diogenes Laertius noted that these shrines still stood on the Areopagus: "Hence even to this day altars may be found . . . *with no name inscribed upon them*, which are memorials of this atonement." So the legacy of Epimenides in Athens was this collection of altars to the unknown god.

His legacy in the wider world, however, was his poetry. In fact, St. Paul quotes one of his poems, citing the author only vaguely as among "some of your poets." What did Epimenides say in his poem? He said: "In him we live and move and have our being" (see Acts 17:28).

St. Paul apparently sees this line as a prophecy of the filial deification—divine sonship that Christians experience through baptism.

His citation is no happenstance. Paul knew the poem well. In fact, he quotes another line from it in his Letter to Titus, the disciple whom he installed as the first bishop of Crete, Epimenides's home. "Cretans," he wrote, "are always liars, evil beasts, lazy gluttons" (Ti 1:12). The line seems different in tone from the one he quoted on the Areopagus, but it comes from the same striking passage, in which King Minos of Crete addresses Zeus, chief among the gods, whom the Cretans thought was mortal.

> They fashioned a tomb for you, holy and high one, Cretans, always liars, evil beasts, lazy gluttons. But you are not dead: you live and abide forever, For in you we live and move and have our being.

Paul knew the poem because he was an educated man, steeped in Hellenistic culture—culture that flowed from sources deep in Athenian history and myth. As he faced a crowd of men who were Athenians and philosophers, Paul could have invoked Plato, whose works he surely knew. He could have invoked Aristotle. He could have argued philosophically. But he did not. Instead he consciously, deliberately invited his hearers to remember a poet, a prophet, a priest, and a lawgiver.

He spoke of a figure crucial to the Athenians' self-understanding—a man whose story was preserved in sources that would have been well known to the educated men on the Areopagus.

To them, Epimenides was a savior figure. First known as a good shepherd, he became a priest, a prophet, and a lawgiver. He had been thought dead, but emerged alive from a cave. He was a foreigner who brought atonement to a people who had been suffering under a curse. He purified them of past sins and taught them the proper way to offer sacrifice—not to the gods, but to *the* god.

Paul didn't make the connections for his listeners, but he assumed that it wasn't necessary. Later in life, as he wrote his Letter to Titus, he recognized Epimenides as a "prophet" (Ti 1:12), a most curious and thought-provoking title to give a non-Israelite.

Archbishop Wojtyła followed the subtle movements of the mind of the apostle. Himself a philosopher, he looked at those long-ago academics on their high place—and surely he saw his twentieth-century colleagues. Yet he notes: "The

Apostle, however, does not enter the path of philosophical conjectures" (II.3).

Instead, St. Paul appealed to the impulses of natural religion. He appealed to the highest form of justice, known to the philosophers, but more primordial than any philosophy. He reminded them, implicitly, that they had known salvation and atonement through sacrifice.

And then he brought it home. Paul spoke to them of the Paschal Mystery, the resurrection of Jesus from the dead.

What are we to make of St. Paul's approach? History looks at the last line of the episode and judges the apostle a failure in this instance: "Some mocked; but others said, 'We will hear you again about this.' . . . But some men joined him and believed, among them Dionysius the Areopagite and a woman named Damaris and others with them" (Acts 17:32, 34).

But did he fail?

The evidence suggests otherwise. Yes, "some" derided him; but we're told that "others" were at least open to listening in the future.

We can also count at least four converts made that day. Two were notable enough to mention by name: Damaris and Dionysius. Tradition tells us that the latter became the first bishop of Athens; and some of the most profound works of Christian mystical literature—the "Dionysian corpus"—bear his name. There were, moreover, still "others with them." "Others" indicates two at minimum, but perhaps even more.

The more we look at chapter 17 of the Acts of the Apostles—especially in the company of a guide like the sainted Archbishop Wojtyła—the less it looks like a failure. It looks to me like a plan.

Works Consulted

Clare K. Rothschild, *Paul in Athens* (Tubingen: Mohr Siebeck, 2014).

William M. Ramsay, *Asianic Elements in Greek Civilisation: The Gifford Lectures in the University of Edinburgh, 1915–16* (London: John Murray, 1927).

ABBREVIATIONS FOR SOURCE DOCUMENTS QUOTED IN THIS WORK

DV   *Dogmatic Constitution on Divine Revelation* (*Dei Verbum*), November 18, 1965

GS   *Pastoral Constitution on the Church in the Modern World* (*Gaudium et Spes*), December 12, 1965

LG   *Dogmatic Constitution on the Church* (*Lumen Gentium*), November 21, 1964

NA   *Declaration on the Relation of the Church to Non-Christian Religions* (*Nostra Aetate*), October 28, 1965

PUBLISHER'S NOTE

The English language edition of this work is presented in a way that attempts to balance the importance of its content with the historical significance of the manuscript as a window into the mind and heart of its author during the fascinating period in which it was written. Therefore, words that were underlined by Archbishop Karol Wojtyła in the original handwritten Polish manuscript have been maintained here and are rendered in *italics* throughout the text.

The epigraphs that begin each teaching were handwritten by Archbishop Wojtyła as inscriptions at the top of each page and are devotional in nature.

All translations and sources are provided by the editor or the translator.

The English translation of *Adoro te devote*, by St. Thomas Aquinas, is based on a common English translation.

The English translation of *Veni, Sancte Spiritus* is from *Lectionary for Mass*, Pentecost Sunday A—Mass During the Day (Collegeville, MN: Liturgical Press, 2000), 482.

The English translation of *Victimae Paschali laudes* is from *Lectionary for Mass*, Easter Sunday—Mass of Easter Day (Collegeville, MN: Liturgical Press, 2000), 348.

SERMON AT THE AREOPAGUS

FROM ACTS 17:16–34

AMDG

J+M

Totus Tuus ego sum
et omnia mea Tua sunt

For the greater glory of God

Jesus and Mary

I am totally yours
and all that is mine is yours

While Paul was waiting for them in Athens, he was deeply distressed to see that the city was full of idols. So he argued in the synagogue with the Jews and the devout persons, and also in the marketplace every day with those who happened to be there. Also some Epicurean and Stoic philosophers debated with him. Some said, "What does this babbler want to say?" Others said, "He seems to be a proclaimer of foreign divinities." (This was because he was telling the good news about Jesus and the resurrection.) So they took him and brought him to the Areopagus and asked him, "May we know what this new teaching is that you are presenting? It sounds rather strange to us, so we would like to know what it means." Now all the Athenians and the foreigners living there would spend their time in nothing but telling or hearing something new.

Then Paul stood in front of the Areopagus and said, "Athenians, I see how extremely religious you are in every way. For as I went through the city and looked carefully at the objects of your worship, I found among them an altar with the inscription, 'To an unknown god.' What therefore you worship as unknown, this I proclaim to you. The God who made the world and everything in it, he who is Lord of heaven and earth, does not live in shrines made by human hands, nor is he served by human hands, as though he needed anything, since he himself gives to all mortals life and breath and all things. From one ancestor he made all nations to inhabit the whole earth, and he allotted the times of their existence and the boundaries of the places where they would live, so that they would search for God and perhaps grope for him and find him—though indeed he is not far from each one of us. For 'In him we live and move and have our being'; as even some of your own poets have said, 'For we too are his offspring.'

"Since we are God's offspring, we ought not to think that the deity is like gold, or silver, or stone, an image formed by the art and imagination of mortals. While God has overlooked the times of human ignorance, now he commands all people everywhere to repent, because he has fixed a day on which he will have the world judged in righteousness by a man whom he has appointed, and of this he has given assurance to all by raising him from the dead."

When they heard of the resurrection of the dead, some scoffed; but others said, "We will hear you again about this." At that point Paul left them. But some of them joined him and became believers, including Dionysius the Areopagite and a woman named Damaris, and others with them.

NOTES

AMDG = Ad maiorem Dei gloriam; *J+M = Jesus et Maria*; "Totus . . ." is from St. Louis de Montfort (1673–1716), expressing consecration of oneself to Mary and was the personal and episcopal motto of Karol Wojtyła/Pope John Paul II for many decades.

I.

"AN UNKNOWN GOD"

Accipio Te in mea omnia
Praebe mihi Cor Tuum, Maria

Victimae Paschali
laudes immolent
christiani

I take you for my all.
Give me your heart, Mary.

Christians, to the Paschal Victim
Offer your thankful praises.

1. In this short cycle of thirteen catecheses, I would like to focus, together with all of you, *on the Areopagus of Athens*, referring to the event described in the Acts of the Apostles. The apostle Paul of Tarsus has recently crossed the border between Asia Minor and Macedonia, setting foot on the European continent for the first time. Arriving in Athens, he finds himself right in the center of the culture, philosophy, art, and religion of the ancient world. This place remains a symbol today, not only of a great past linked to Greece and Athens, but also a symbol of what has endured for centuries and generations. The entire *culture of Europe*, of Western civilization, *comes from there*: from Greek culture, from the Areopagus—as from a spring.

2. Therefore, this chapter from the Acts of the Apostles constitutes the ideal background for these catecheses addressed to the people of our time. Moreover, the person who speaks in this place—*Paul of Tarsus*—not only represents history but also is a symbol. He, a Pharisee who converted to Christ, who had previously persecuted the nascent Church, speaking at the Areopagus, testifies to *the encounter of the spiritual heritage of Israel with the heritage of Greece*. We come from this double heritage. So, deepening the theme of the catechesis cycle in progress, we will also have the opportunity to return to *our spiritual origins*.

3. We read in the Acts of the Apostles that Paul, having arrived in Athens, "was deeply distressed to see that the city was full of idols" (Acts 17:16). His indignation is understandable, given that he had grown up from childhood

in a climate of rigorous monotheism. However, when he begins to speak standing in the middle of the Areopagus, he does not show indignation. On the contrary, he expresses appreciation to the Athenians for their belief: "I see how *extremely religious you are* in every way" (Acts 17:22). The apostle is prompted to begin with this expression not so much because he has seen all the signs of Athenian polytheism, but because in addition to the many places dedicated to the cults of various gods, he has also found an altar with the inscription *"To an unknown god"* (Acts 17:23).

4. Perhaps we, too, should stop in front of this altar. Certainly, it is the right place to reflect not only on the religion of ancient Greece, but also on the phenomenon and on the factor of religion in general. Here we let the Fathers of the Second Vatican Council speak; they addressed the subject of religion authoritatively, taking into particular consideration non-Christian religions. In *the words of the Declaration Nostra Aetate*: "Men expect from the various religions answers to the unsolved riddles of the human condition, which today, even as in former times, deeply stir the hearts of men: What is man? What is the meaning, the aim of our life? What is moral good, what is sin? Whence suffering and what purpose does it serve? Which is the road to true happiness? What are death, judgment and retribution after death? What, finally, is that ultimate inexpressible mystery which encompasses our existence: whence do we come, and where are we going?" (*NA*, 1).

5. Contemporary scholars who study the phenomenon of religion in its many aspects give great attention to *the value of the "sacred,"* which seems to constitute the core of religious experience. The words of Paul at the Areopagus, as well as the aforementioned text of the conciliar document, highlight above all the meaning of religion. *Religion is the search for answers to the fundamental questions about human existence.* These questions concern "border" problems, where human knowledge, based on sensory experience, finds itself facing unanswered questions. All these questions bring us closer to that Mystery which is "ultimate" and "inexpressible." The apostle Paul, speaking on the Areopagus, says: "so that they would search for God and perhaps grope for him and find him" (Acts 17:27).

6. And so the Athenian altar with the inscription "To an unknown god" is for the Apostle of Tarsus an expression of religion (and belief): *religion as a search for God.* In the council declaration we read: "From ancient times down to the present, there is found among various peoples *a certain perception of that hidden power* which hovers over the course of things and over the events of human history; at times some indeed have come to the recognition of a Supreme Being, or even of a Father. This perception and recognition penetrates their lives with a profound religious sense. Religions, however, that are bound up with an advanced culture have struggled to answer the same questions by means of more refined concepts and a more developed language" (*NA*, 2).

At this point, the council mentions *Hinduism* and *Buddhism*, with a brief description of both religious systems. What is said about them applies to other religions, as all "try to counter *the restlessness of the human heart*, each in its own manner" (*NA*, 2). These words on the "restlessness of the heart" immediately recall the famous expression of Augustine of Hippo. He was particularly sensitive to these anxieties of the human heart that point to the "ultimate inexpressible Mystery" that is God.

The conciliar text to which we refer speaks of *religion as a dimension of human existence in the world*. In this dimension, religion is the expression of a search that goes beyond what is visible, toward an "unknown God," as the inscription on the Athenian altar demonstrates. For the apostle Paul, this inscription was the proof of the Athenians' religious belief more than all the statues of the gods he had seen on other altars. In this way, the ancient Greek tried to express his religious sense.

It is known that the religion of the Greeks of that time was *linked to a rich mythology with decidedly anthropomorphic features*. One can say that in this traditional religion of the people, humankind had created gods (idols) according to human imagination.

This is why Paul, as we read, "was deeply distressed" (Acts 17:16). Only the altar dedicated to an "unknown god" met his approval. He, *the apostle of that "unknown" God*, referred to this in the first words of his speech at the Areopagus: "What therefore you worship as unknown, this I proclaim to you" (Acts 17:23).

Before continuing with our considerations, let us add again what we read in the declaration on non-Christian religions: "The Catholic Church rejects nothing that is true and holy in these religions. She regards with sincere reverence those ways of conduct and of life . . . which . . . *often reflect a ray of that Truth* which enlightens all men" (*NA*, 2). The ancient Christian writers, in this regard, did not hesitate to speak of "seeds of the Word" (*semina Verbi*).[1]

NOTES

The monogram, ☧, is an ancient symbol of Jesus Christ that is made up of the first two Greek letters—*chi* and *rho*—of the word Χριϛτος ("Christ") superimposed and was, along with AMDG and J+M, inscribed at the left corner of each handwritten page as a devotional practice; "*Accipio Te . . .*" is a continuation of the motto from St. Louis de Montfort; "*Victimae . . .*" here Archbishop Wojtyła begins inscribing the top of the handwritten pages with some lines from the text of the *Victimae Paschali laudes*, the traditional Gospel Sequence for Easter Sunday.

1. The expression *semina Verbi* is taken from St. Justin and St. Clement of Alexandria; it appears in Eusebius of Caesarea's *Praeparatio evangelica* and indicates the traces of Christ present in creation: the Christian faith teaches that the Father created the world in Christ through the Holy Spirit.

II.

"THE ONE
WHO IS"

Agnus
redemit oves
Christus innocens
Patri
reconciliavit peccatores

A Lamb the sheep redeems;
Christ, who only is sinless,
Reconciles sinners to the Father.

the "moment" of the beginning. That is, the moment before which its existence cannot be demonstrated, and therefore: the moment from which it all began. How? In accordance with their cognitive principles, the natural sciences do not speak of creation. We, however, dwelling at the Athenian Areopagus, can say that the apostle Paul, even from the point of view of the modern knowledge of the cosmos, does not encounter any significant obstacle in speaking of "the God who made the world and everything that is in it." Of the God in whom "we live and move and have our being."

Of the One who IS.

NOTES

"*Agnus . . .*" is from the Easter Sunday Gospel Sequence *Victimae Paschali laudes.*

III.

THE HUMAN BEING AND TRUTH

Mors et vita
duello conflixere mirando
Dux vitae
mortuus
regnat vivus
Dic nobis Maria

Death and life have contended in that com-
bat stupendous:
The Prince of life, who died, reigns
immortal.
Speak Mary

1. A God in whom "we live and move and have our being." The words of the apostle Paul spoken at the Athenian Areopagus are extremely significant. They reveal *the majesty of the existence of God*: *the world* and everything in it *exists in God*. At the same time God is not "outside" the world. If "in him we live and move and have our being," it means that God also constitutes the intimate mystery of creation. In the very fact of "creation," there is a reference to the Creator. The philosopher will say: in the contingency of the essence (non-necessity) is the reference to the Absolute.[1]

2. If God constitutes the inner mystery of every creature, this particularly concerns the human person. Speaking at the Areopagus, the apostle connects this truth above all *to humankind*. "In him (in God) we live and move and have our being," and he adds, "as even some of your own poets have said, *'For we too are his offspring.'*" As we can see, Paul knew not only philosophy, but also Greek poetry. In fact, there are poets in which such expressions are found (e.g., Cleanthes: *Hymn to Zeus*, and similarly Aratus of Soli in Cilicia). The pedagogical method of the apostle, his ability to root the evangelical *kerygma*[2] in the culture of the place, should be admired.

Although the concept of "seeds of the Word" (*semina Verbi*) is expressed later in the Hellenistic world by the thinkers of early Christianity, we can see that it was not unfamiliar to Paul of Tarsus. The apostle is also the pioneer of "inculturation."

3. Indeed, the Greek poets, expressing the conviction that the human race is "the offspring of God," *touched the truth of biblical revelation* (probably without knowing it). In the book of Genesis, in the context of the description of the creation of the world from nothing, there is a phrase that emphasizes the extraordinary relationship between the Creator and the creature that is human. "*So God created humankind* in his image; *in the image of God he created them*; male and female he created them" (Gn 1:27). God created human beings (as shown in the entire biblical story) when there were suitable conditions, to be able to give them the land as a dwelling and at the same time as a responsibility. Saying: "Let us make humankind in our image, according to our likeness" (Gn 1:26), the Creator revealed the fullness of his creative act, not only with regard to the future evolution of the visible world, but also (and above all) *in the light of the eternal divine plan* concerning the human being in the created world. But the book of Genesis does not yet speak of it openly. This will only appear in the scriptures of the New Testament (e.g., cf. Eph 1:3). The eternal divine plan concerning humankind, and indirectly all creation, "will be revealed" only by Jesus Christ.

4. When the apostle says to the Athenians: "for we too are his offspring," he certainly is thinking of the truth about our creation in the image and likeness of God, but not only this. *Being "God's offspring"* means not only "being created," remaining in relationship with God as well as all other created (and "contingent") beings. Being God's offspring means *"to be begotten."* This expression, borrowed from

pagan poetry, penetrates deeply into the mystery of adoption as God's children, made possible for humanity thanks to Christ, the Son who is consubstantial with the Father: to them "he gave power to become children of God" (Jn 1:12), as the evangelist John proclaimed in the prologue of his gospel.

5. In the creation of humankind in the image and likeness of God, "the adoption as his children" is written in the Eternal Son, who is also the "firstborn of all creation" (cf. Col 1:15). With the creation of humankind in the image of God, *the perspective of participation in the nature of God* (cf. 2 Pt 1:4), *in the interior life of God*, opens up. The history of humankind in the world becomes the history of salvation through grace: "through Christ, the Word made flesh, man might in the Holy Spirit have access to the Father and come to share in the divine nature (see Eph 2:18; 2 Pt 1:4)" (cf. *DV*, 2). All this is indicated by the words "we too are his offspring."

6. The whole truth about the human person is constituted by the gifts of nature and of supernatural grace. The human being, as the image and likeness of God, is a rational being. In his humanity he combines corporeality, sensuality, and spirituality. Through spirituality, the person surpasses (transcends) in an asymmetrical way the whole world of living beings. From the very beginning he was placed in the visible cosmos "above" them. *Spirituality means rationality and freedom*: two qualities that make humankind already similar to God "by nature."

7. Through reason, *all existence is given to humankind in truth*: as truth. Rationality is not just the ability to form (reproduce) objects in a sensitive way. It is the capacity, and also the task, of "communing" with them in truth. The relationship with the whole in truth and through truth constitutes an essential characteristic of spirituality, in which the sensory dimension of knowledge is overcome absolutely. While the senses capture the material objects in a perceptive (and also, indirectly, imaginative) way in their singularity, *the intellect-reason seeks the whole and the totality*. Therefore it must be said that in the intellect-reason the human being has been given all that exists (in whatever form): all that is created, the universe, and even God. Hence the "search for God" that St. Paul speaks of at the Areopagus. This search constitutes the *rational foundation of every religion*. Even if "groping" (cf. Acts 17:27) (as the apostle says) is, however, pervaded by the intimate aspiration to know the truth about God. We can therefore say that every religion is "intentionally" open to the Truth that is God, although this truth finds in different (historical) religions an expression that is inadequate and at times even wrong.

8. In order for God to be known in truth, *he must let himself be known by human reason*. The human mind is able not only to seek the truth about God through the created world, but also to "listen to the voice of God" above the voice of creatures. Here we touch on a matter that is important for the objective truthfulness of religion. In the human mind lies *the disposition of listening (potentia oboedientialis) to the inner voice of God*: the truth about him, which he alone

knows and which he expresses "intimately" in the eternal Word. When this "interior discourse" of God is directed "outside himself" to rational creatures, humankind becomes a *witness to God's self-revelation*. This self-revelation of God is inscribed in the history of creation, and in particular in human history from the beginning (from the first three chapters of the book of Genesis).

In the Letter to the Hebrews we read: "Long ago God spoke to our ancestors in many and various ways by the prophets, but in these last days he has spoken to us by a Son. . . . He is the reflection of God's glory and the exact imprint of God's very being" (Heb 1:1–3). In the prologue of John, we read: "In the beginning was the Word, and the Word was with God, and the Word was God" (Jn 1:1). "And the Word became flesh" (Jn 1:14). The Creator has given the human being a created existence. Through human reason he gave him the world as truth. *He also revealed himself— intimate Divine Mystery—to humankind in the Word made flesh.*

The truth of religion is substantially linked to this Word. Humanity's relationship with God—and consequently with creatures—is a relationship in truth and matures in listening to this Word. In the "obedience of faith."

We need not fear this word: the disposition to listen to the Truth (that is, obedience) and the readiness to act in the Truth constitute the true dignity of the human person.

NOTES

"*Mors . . .*" is from the Easter Sunday Gospel Sequence *Victimae Paschali laudes*; "Maria" here refers to Mary Magdalene. The verse asks her to recount what she saw at the tomb of Christ on Easter morning.

1. Cf. the third philosophical *via* (way) of demonstrating the existence of God in St. Thomas Aquinas, *Summa Theologiae*, I-I, qu. 2, art. 3.

2. A Greek word meaning the kernel or core message of the Christian faith: Jesus Christ—the Incarnate Son of God who died and rose from the dead for us—is Lord.

IV.

THE HUMAN BEING AND FREEDOM

quid vidisti
in via
Sepulcrum
Christi viventis
et gloriam vidi resurgentis
Angelicos testes

What you saw, wayfaring.
"The tomb of Christ, who is living,
The glory of Jesus' resurrection;
Bright angels attesting."

1. In the next catecheses, we will try to develop the themes contained in the apostolic catechesis of St. Paul. It is a particular *kerygma*. The apostle refers to the altar with the inscription "To an unknown god" that the Athenians included among the places of worship dedicated to the gods of their polytheistic religion. *Speaking of this "unknown" God*, who is the One God, Creator of all that exists and Lord of heaven and earth, *the apostle develops the anthropological theme in parallel*. He speaks of the human being as God's "offspring." This expression of the pagan poet helps the speaker not only to enter into the biblical truth about the creation of the human being—man and woman—in the image and likeness of God, but at the same time it allows him to refer to the revealed mystery of humanity's "adoption as children" in Christ. Admittedly, the apostle does not develop this truth at the Areopagus—yet we know that he did so in his magnificent letters which are *an inexhaustible source of knowledge about God's economy of salvation in human history*.

2. Before we go into these essential topics in further catecheses, let us stop once again at this similarity with God in which human beings participate "by nature." Every human being created in the image of God is a rational and free person. *Rationality and freedom* are the two fundamental properties of an individual, the properties of the human spirit. By means of rationality—a property of the intellect of the individual subject—the Creator "consigns" the whole of reality in terms of truth (as previously stated), so this *same reality is consigned to the human being in terms of*

good: as good. This responsibility is inscribed in the nature and constitution of the person through a will that is free. Freedom as a characteristic of the person is directly related to the will. If *the will in itself is a pursuit of the previously known good (pre-cognitum)*, freedom discerns this pursuit among all the aspirations, inclinations, and desires that in the world of living beings are defined by the term *appetitus.*[1] The will therefore constitutes the *appetitus rationalis;*[2] it is the pursuit proper to a rational being, and that means it remains *essential and internal to the truth.*

3. Therefore all of reality—the whole world of goods available through the senses and through reason—has been given and entrusted to the human being from the beginning, in this intimate relationship, in relation to the truth. *Thanks to this relationship, the human will is free.* The human being, as an image of God, is capable of self-determination. In this sense, he is a "sovereign" subject. If the human being must govern the visible world and must choose from among the creatures an inferior nature that the Creator has entrusted to him from the beginning (cf. Gn 1:28–29), the foundation of this power lies within his own humanity: *self-control (mastery of self) is the first expression of freedom* as self-determination. The free action of the human being turns "outward" to known goods, but at the same time it penetrates the interior self and imprints a profound seal there which affects the whole person. The human being, by his own agency, with his own actions, by virtue of their freedom, *becomes good or bad as an individual*: good or bad *in a moral sense.* Morality is immanently

linked to the freedom of the acting subject, and the moral qualification—good or evil—confirms the relationship of freedom to the truth; but even more: it confirms the organic dependence of freedom on the truth, which constitutes *the very dynamic core of the personal being.* That being which is in the image and likeness of God.

4. An analysis of the human act of will indicates moments that do not appear throughout the *appetitus* of the animal world. An act of will can be a simple conscious wish, but more often the will is revealed *as a choice and a decision.* The entire inner process of the will is guided by the awareness of the *nihil volitum nisi praecognitum,*[3] that is to say, by the relation of the truth to the good and by internal dependence on this truth. This dependence does not undermine freedom; on the contrary, it defines and liberates it. Christ's words on the truth that sets us free (cf. Jn 8:32) are confirmed by the very intrinsic structure of the acts of the human will: *dependence on the truth determines the freedom of the will and its individual subject.* This explains the close *link between freedom and responsibility* (first of all in a moral sense). The human person, created as an individual, is responsible for his own actions. Responsibility means that the whole personal agency of a human being and its effects depend on the truth concerning the good.

5. All this is revealed through the analysis of the intrinsic act of the will as a factor that constitutes the whole essentially human action of the person. This anthropological truth in the Pauline sermon at the Areopagus is closely

connected to what the apostle says of the "unknown God": the Creator who is the Lord of heaven and earth. This God, as we will hear later, "commands all people everywhere to repent, because he has fixed a day on which he will have the world judged in righteousness" (Acts 17:30–31).

The truth about the one God, who as the Creator and Lord is the just Judge of good and evil, is the primary content of the Christian faith, monotheism, and in a certain sense of any religion. Therefore, what the apostle proclaims does not prompt any objection from his Athenian listeners. *God—just Judge*—the one who ultimately will be able to judge the good and the evil of all, of often complicated human affairs, at the same time *attests to how fundamental the question of whether a person's actions are good or evil is to the person himself.* The human being is conscious of his freedom and the responsibility associated with it, which is ultimately a responsibility toward God.

Before the one who is Omniscience and Wisdom, "everything is naked and uncovered": transparent in its intrinsic truth. In the internal human dimension, *the truth of actions belongs to conscience.* As the supreme Judge, God—and he alone—is the judge of human consciences.

6. The apostle says, however, that God "will have the world judged." Here, then, this personal and strictly internal affair of every human being has at the same time a cosmic and macroscopic dimension. In effect, the history of the world, of human communities and societies, the history of all humanity, depends on that good and evil of which each person is the author. In our age, especially, much is said

about *the social dimensions of morality*. There is also talk of the *structures of sin* which, in a wide range, condition the moral life of entire societies, nations, and continents.

When all this is made present before our eyes, the assertion that *God has entrusted to the human being*—as a person and as a community, as an individual and as a collective— that reality which is called "world" *as good* takes on a more complete meaning. Each one of us has received from the Creator his own humanity and that of others. It has been given to us in truth and in goodness. But this truth eventually arrives at God himself who is the Fullness of the Good, as attested to by the greatest commandment of the Gospel: *you will love.*

7. Regarding this task—at the level of the entire spiritual cosmos—*a fundamental fracture and opposition* has occurred: on the one hand, the love *Dei usque ad contemptum sui*, and on the other, the love *sui usque ad contemptum Dei*,[4] as the great Augustine of Hippo says.

So deep is the *drama of freedom* in the history of the visible and invisible world.

However, God creates the human being both rational and free, wanting above all to express his image and likeness in the human person. Even at the cost of abusing the great gift of freedom.

Notes

"*quid vidisti . . .*" is from the Easter Sunday Gospel Sequence *Victimae Paschali laudes.*

1. Latin for "desire, longing, appetite."

2. Rational or reasonable desire.

3. Latin maxim that translates "nothing is desired unless it is first known."

4. These Latin phrases translate as "of God to the point of indifference toward self" and "of self to the point of indifference toward God" (Augustine of Hippo, *De Civitate Dei*, 14, 28: CSEL 40, 2, 56).

V.

THE TRUTH
OF THE
RESURRECTION

sudarium et vestes
Surrexit Christus
spes mea
praecedet suos
in Galilaeam

Veni Sancte Spiritus

The shroud and napkin resting.
Yes, Christ my hope is arisen;
To Galilee he goes before you.

Come Holy Spirit

1. "While God has overlooked the times of human igno-rance, now he commands all people everywhere to repent, because he has *fixed a day on which he will have the world judged in righteousness.*" These are the words spoken by the apostle Paul at the Athenian Areopagus to the experts in Greek poetry and philosophy, in particular of the Stoic and Epicurean schools, who were eager to listen to "something new." As before, they listen attentively and without objec-tion to what the apostle says. The truth about God, the cre-ator of the world and of humankind, the God "in whom we live and move and have our being," seems to have met with their approval.

But here Paul touches the topic of Jesus Christ. He says: "God . . . has fixed a day on which he will have the world judged in righteousness by a man whom he has appointed, and of this he has given assurance to all by raising him from the dead" (Acts 17:31).

2. *At this point, opposition breaks out.* "When they heard of the resurrection of the dead, some scoffed; but others said, 'We will hear you again about this'" (Acts 17:32). The author of the Acts of the Apostles adds: "At that point Paul left them." This is neither the first nor the only incident in which the apostolic *kerygma* encounters resistance.

There are also other places on the Pauline journey where listeners *do not want to accept the truth about the crucified and risen Christ.* The Athenian incident, however, is unique. Resistance to the proclamation of the Gospel in this case does not come from people who knew the Old Testament and lived within the context of the Israelite tradition. The

Athenians represent a completely different world of religious concepts. The apostle's listeners who belonged to the Israelite tradition knew the truth about God, who revealed himself to the people by making a covenant with their fathers. *For the Athenians,* however, *religion was above all the expression of man-made traditions.* Hellenic people had devised a polytheistic mythology that expressed itself in a popular piety. Some, like the intellectuals and the philosophers, independently of this popular religion, sought to give a purely rational answer to the question of the Absolute.

3. This state of the environment is explained by the whole structure of the Pauline *kerygma* at the Areopagus. In environments linked to the tradition of the faith of Israel, the apostles—and especially Paul—expressed themselves differently. Nevertheless, in both cases, *the Paschal Mystery of Jesus Christ is always found at the center of the apostolic kerygma.* The other apostles had witnessed this mystery. Through the women, going to the sepulcher the day after the Passover sabbath to anoint the body of Jesus of Nazareth entombed there, they received the news of the stone rolled away and the empty tomb. "Why do you seek the living one among the dead? He is not here, but he has been raised" (cf. Lk 24:5–6). In turn, the apostles personally discovered that the tomb was empty.

4. This event, however, did not end with this "negative proof." *The Resurrection of Christ has been confirmed in a positive way.* Paul writes about this (in a very concise way, it seems) in the First Letter to the Corinthians: "For I handed

on to you as of first importance what I in turn had received: *that* Christ *died for our sins in accordance with the scriptures, and that he was buried, and that he was raised on the third day in accordance with the scriptures, and that he appeared to Cephas, then to the twelve.* Then he appeared to more than five hundred brothers and sisters at one time, most of whom are still alive, though some have died. Then he appeared to James, then to all the apostles. Last of all, as to one untimely born, he appeared also to me" (1 Cor 15:3–8). This passage from the letter to the Corinthians is considered one of the oldest catechetical texts of the New Testament. As you can see, the content of this catechesis (*kerygma*) is *the truth about Christ: his redemptive death* ("for our sins"), *his burial in the tomb, and the Resurrection.* The apostles are witnesses to all these events that make up the Paschal Mystery of Christ: the key content of the faith of all Christians.

5. To the various Christophanies of the Risen Lord, finally, Paul adds the one he himself experienced *at the gates of Damascus.* We know that this experience completely transformed him. Saul dies and Paul is born in his place. Saul was the fierce enemy of the Name of Christ; Paul became his ardent apostle.

In the words spoken at the Athenian Areopagus—on the basis of the extraordinary discourse on the "unknown God"—the truth about the Resurrection of Christ appears as a culminating point and at the same time a *crowning* of the entire *kerygma. The apostle testifies that this "unknown God,"* the only Creator and Lord of all creation, who (in the end) "will have the world judged in righteousness" has revealed himself in the fullness of time *in Christ*. In him he became known as the true Lord of life and death, Lord of all that exists, "The ONE who IS." He has revealed himself, irrevocably and definitively, in the *Resurrection*. To the Jews Christ had said: "When you have lifted up the Son of Man, then you will realize that I am he" (Jn 8:28). He means, you will know that I am the "ONE who IS": that I am of the same substance as the Father.

6. Speaking at the Areopagus, the apostle does everything possible to prepare and approach listeners who do not know the true name of God, written in the history of the Old Covenant (from the time of Moses), for this key truth of the New Covenant: the Resurrection. *The Resurrection* presupposes true death; *it forms a whole with the redemptive death of Christ on the Cross*. In this same Letter to the Corinthians, Paul writes: "For Jews demand signs and Greeks desire wisdom, but we proclaim Christ crucified, a stumbling block to Jews and foolishness to Gentiles, but to those who are the called, both Jews and Greeks, Christ the power of God and the wisdom of God. For God's foolishness is wiser than human wisdom, and God's weakness is stronger than human strength" (1 Cor 1:22–25).

7. At the Areopagus of Athens, the apostle does not speak of the Cross, but concentrates on the Resurrection. The Resurrection, however, is inseparable from the Cross, just as the Cross—death on the Cross—is inseparable from the Resurrection. It is precisely *the Resurrection that confirms the power of God and the wisdom of God expressed in the*

Cross of Christ. These events, united together, constitute the Paschal Mystery. The apostle proclaims the Paschal Mystery as the "being or not being" of the faith of the Church: of Christian existence in faith!

We read: "And if Christ has not been raised, then our proclamation has been in vain and your faith has been in vain" (1 Cor 15:14). "But in fact Christ has been raised from the dead, the first fruits of those who have died. For since death came through a human being, the resurrection of the dead has also come through a human being; for as all die in Adam, so all will be made alive in Christ" (1 Cor 15:20–22).

8. This key and central truth of the Pauline *kerygma*—the definitive Word about the "unknown God" to human-kind—met with doubt, unbelief, and rejection in Athens. The apostle was defeated by the Greeks who "seek wisdom." However, "some of them joined him and became believers, including Dionysius the Areopagite and a woman named Damaris, and others with them" (Acts 17:34).

Almost two thousand years later, *the Second Vatican Council declares*: "The Church firmly believes that Christ, who died and was raised up for all, can through His Spirit offer man the light and the strength to measure up to his supreme destiny. Nor has any other name under the heaven been given to man by which it is fitting for him to be saved. She likewise holds that in her most benign Lord and Master can be found the key, the focal point and the goal of man, as well as of all human history" (*GS*, 10).

NOTES

"*sudarium et . . .*" is from the Easter Sunday Gospel Sequence *Victimae Paschali laudes*; "*Veni . . .*": Here Archbishop Wojtyła begins inscribing some lines from the text of *Veni, Sancte Spiritus*, the traditional Gospel sequence for Pentecost Sunday.

VI.

THE MYSTERY OF THE INCARNATION

et emitte coelitus
Lucis tuae radium
Veni, Pater pauperum
Veni Dator munerum
veni, lumen cordium
Consolator optime

and from your celestial home
Shed a ray of light divine!
Come, Father of the poor!
Come, source of all our store!
Come, within our bosoms shine!
You, of comforters the best.

1. "When they heard of the resurrection of the dead, some scoffed; but others said, 'We will hear you again about this.'" The apostle's listeners at the Athenian Areopagus *rejected the truth about the Resurrection of Christ* he proclaimed. As long as he spoke of that "unknown god" to whom they had dedicated an altar in Athens, they remained to listen to him. But they did not accept the truth about the Resurrection. The truth about the immortality of the soul was familiar to Greek thought. According to Plato's teachings, the spiritual soul constitutes in itself the human being, while the body is only a temporary prison. Perhaps it was for this reason that *the "resurrection of the body" seemed so contrary to their understanding of the human person.* Platonic anthropology differs from the Christian one. At the center of the Gospel is the truth about the Resurrection (as was mentioned in the previous catechesis), and this truth indicates that the body together with the soul co-create the essence of the human person.

2. Thus, one can say that the failure of the Pauline *kerygma* in Athens was caused by a different understanding of human nature. For the apostle, the question of humankind is deeply rooted in the truth about the "unknown God" he proclaimed: "What therefore you worship as unknown, this I proclaim to you" (Acts 17:23). This is the *God who "so loved the world that he gave his only Son,* so that everyone who believes in him may not perish but may have eternal life" (cf. Jn 3:16). These words of Christ (in the conversation with Nicodemus) capture the very core of the gospel truth about God.

3. For the apostle's Athenian listeners, such a God was "unknown." Unknown and *incomprehensible was a God who loves*. Love was understood as a pursuit of the good that corresponds to the needs of the human being. "Eros" is a pursuit that is able to assume (as in Plato) a spiritual character, becoming a search for goodness, truth, and beauty. In contrast, the truth about a love that creates good, bestows it, and by virtue of this elevates the human being, ennobles him, and makes him happy was alien. That is why the God of Paul was an "unknown" God. The God who loves the world, who *gives himself to everyone* in this world *in the only-begotten Son*: he gives because he is above all *Love*. Such a God was "unknown" and incomprehensible. To understand him, a "spiritual coup" was necessary, one which did not happen in the Athenians who heard Paul, with the exception of the few mentioned in the Acts of the Apostles.

4. The Gospel, the whole New Covenant, is a written *Testimony about* this *God who revealed himself in Jesus Christ*, his Son. The Old Covenant was the preparation for this definitive testimony that God spoke in the Word made flesh. "The law indeed was given through Moses; grace and truth came through Jesus Christ" (cf. Jn 1:17). "*Grace and truth*": the Only-begotten Son not only "revealed" God whom "no one has ever seen" (cf. Jn 1:18); but in him this infinite God gave himself; he gave human beings the possibility of participating in the Divine nature; he gave them "eternal life," that is, salvation. This gift is called grace.

5. "For God so loved the world." The Resurrection of Christ, which the apostle proclaimed to the Athenians, was only the last Word of this intervention, of *this "trespassing" of the invisible God into the visible world*, and in particular into human history. The acceptance of this truth opened up a completely new horizon in human consciousness. It brought about a profound transformation of human existence: a saving transformation. Religion as cult (of some utilitarian importance) gave way to faith in the Love that embraces the human person and is the only thing capable of saving him.

In the Gospel, on one hand, God reveals himself to humankind *as "one who gives himself"* to the creature made in his image and likeness. On the other hand, by virtue of this self-revelation of God, *the human being knows himself as being able to* "transcend" himself to the point of becoming a participant in the divine nature.

6. *"But when the fullness of time had come, God sent his Son, born of a woman,* born under the law, in order to redeem those who were under the law, so that we might receive adoption as children" (Gal 4:4–5). These words of Paul in the Letter to the Galatians express that same truth about God that Christ revealed in his nocturnal conversation with Nicodemus: "God so loved the world that he gave his only Son." The apostle writes: "he sent." *This "sending"* (that is, *missio*: mission) of the Son who is consubstantial with the Father reached *its historical* (but also eschatological) *zenith in the mystery of the Incarnation.* The Incarnation means the ultimate fulfillment of God's "giving of himself"

to humankind. On the part of human beings, it is also the culmination and fullness of that "self-transcending" to participation in the divine being. And it is for this reason that the woman, chosen by God as the Mother of the Only-begotten One in the mystery of the Incarnation, hears at the moment of the Annunciation the words "full of grace."

7. This greeting is the introduction to the proclamation in which *the trinitarian mystery of God* is *revealed* for the first time. The angel says: "Do not be afraid, Mary, for you have found favor with God. And now, you will conceive in your womb and bear a son, and you will name him Jesus. He will be great, and will be called the Son of the Most High." And when Mary asks: "How can this be, since I am a virgin?" she receives the following answer: "The Holy Spirit will come upon you, and the power of the Most High will overshadow you; therefore the child to be born will be holy; he will be called Son of God" (Lk 1:30–32, 34, 35).

8. The announcing angel transmits to Mary *the content of God's eternal plan* as *the will of the Father*. When the Virgin responds: "let it be with me according to your word," the mystery of the Incarnation of the Word, Son consubstantial with the Father, is accomplished ("the Word became flesh," Jn 1:14). At the same time, the Virgin of Nazareth is the first creature to whom God reveals the Trinitarian mystery of his divinity. That "*unknown God*," whom the apostle wanted to announce to the Athenians at the Areopagus, is the divine Unity of the Father, the Son, and the Holy Spirit. God—One in the absolute divine unity, and also One in the ineffable

mystery of the Trinity. One—in the eternal Communion of Persons (only in this way can the truth about God be expressed, at the limits of human language and of faculties of the human mind in the face of the mystery of the Living God).

9. At Ain Karem,[1] upon meeting Mary, Elizabeth will say to her: "*blessed is she who believed*" (Lk 1:45). Believing means accepting the truth expressed in the Word of God and therefore opening the human mind to the Truth which is divine in its essence. Faith involves the participation of the human mind in knowledge which is God's own. At the beginning of the New Covenant of God with humanity, Mary is the first among believers, just as Abraham had become "the father of believers" at the beginning of the Old Covenant.

10. "*What therefore you worship as unknown, this I proclaim to you,*" says Paul to the Athenians, referring to the altar dedicated to the unknown God. This "unknown" and ineffable God whom "no one has ever seen" (Jn 1:18) is the Eternal One—Father, Son, and Holy Spirit. But this is also the God who, in the fullness of time, sent the Son "born of a woman" to redeem (ransom) people burdened by the inheritance of sin. The apostle writes of those who were "under the Law," and so alludes therefore mainly to the sons and daughters of Israel. While *the Old Covenant* manifested itself *with the Law* (given to Moses at the foot of Mount Sinai), *the New Covenant manifests itself in "adoption as children"* (that is, in "grace and truth") through the Son made

human. The apostle writes: "And because you are children, God has sent the Spirit of his Son into our hearts, crying, 'Abba! Father'" (Gal 4:6). "Abba, Father"—this is how Jesus Christ addressed God himself. He alone.

NOTES

"*et emitte . . .*" is from the Pentecost Sunday Gospel Sequence, *Veni, Sancte Spiritus.*

1. The village in Palestine where, according to tradition, St. Zechariah and St. Elizabeth, the parents of St. John the Baptist, lived.

VII.

THE MYSTERY OF REDEMPTION

Dulcis Hospes animae
Dulce Refrigerium.
In labore Requies
in fletu Solacium
O lux beatissima
reple cordis intima

You, the soul's most welcome guest;
Sweet refreshment here below;
In our labor, rest most sweet;
Solace in the midst of woe.
O most blessed Light divine,
Shine within these hearts of yours.

1. At the Areopagus, the apostle Paul announces the risen *Christ, whom God "has appointed" as judge* (cf. Acts 17:31). All, then, are called to conversion, because God "has fixed a day on which he will have the world judged in righteousness" through him. The certainty of God's judgment is a fundamental religious truth. Connected to this judgment is the notion of absolute justice, which humankind does not find in the earthly world. *Earthly life is not sufficient for the realization of justice* for both the evil and the good of human deeds and human destiny.

In his Athens speech, the apostle links the question of God's just judgment to the mission of Christ, and in particular to the Resurrection. Raising him from the dead, God has confirmed Christ's right to be "judge of the living and the dead" (cf. Acts 10:42).

2. Just as in the previous catechesis, we refer here to the words of Jesus in the conversation with Nicodemus: *"Indeed, God did not send the Son into the world to condemn the world, but in order that the world might be saved through him"* (Jn 3:17). And so the God who reveals himself in Jesus Christ is above all a God of salvation. The very name of Jesus (*Yeshu'a*—God who saves) speaks of it. And he is the God of salvation because he is "Love" (cf. 1 Jn 4:8). He is Love in the intimate mystery of his divinity as Trinity, or "communion" of Father, Son, and Holy Spirit. From this Trinitarian source also originates the fact that "God so loved the world." He loved it so much that he gave his only Son "that the world might be saved through him" (Jn 3:16–17).

This *soteriological truth* (the truth about God who saves) *does not "invalidate" the truth about God's judgment.* It is the judgment that "the Father has given to the Son" (cf. Jn 5:22) sending him for the salvation of the world. In this context, however, the same truth about God's judgment takes on a new meaning. Jesus says: "And this is the judgment, that the light has come into the world . . . those who do what is true come to the light, so that it may be clearly seen that their deeds have been done in God" (Jn 3:19–21).

3. Here we stand before the mystery of justice "reconciled" with love. At the same time, we face the mystery of love in which all justice finds its perfect fulfillment. *God himself is this "reconciliation" of justice with love.* We find this fundamental truth about God in the long series of statements of the Old Testament, and in particular in the Prophets. However, the ultimate and definitive expression of this truth is the self-revelation of God in Jesus Christ. All that Jesus "did" and "taught" testifies to the "reconciliation" of justice with love in the dimension of God himself, just as *the Cross and the Resurrection constitute its supreme witness.*

In the paschal events, *the mystery of Redemption* is revealed. In the power of this mystery, the world is saved by the Son whom the Father "sent into the world" (cf. Jn 3:17).

4. Thus, between the truth about perfect justice, which is God himself, and the judgment as an act of this justice, stands the mystery of Redemption. The Resurrection of Christ, which the apostle proclaimed at the Athenian Areopagus, is the confirmation and, one can say, the "crowning"

of this mystery realized *in the power of the Cross of Christ on Golgotha*. As the Son of God, Christ was so powerful as to "bear upon the cross" (cf. 1 Pt 2:24) the sin of humankind in its universal dimension. "For our sake he made him to be sin who knew no sin"—we read in the Second Letter to the Corinthians (2 Cor 5:21). In Isaiah, *the Songs of the Servant of YHWH*, many centuries before the paschal event on Golgotha, prepared the ground for this otherwise unbelievable reality.

5. *The history of freedom*, which the Creator gave to man as a being in his image and likeness, has developed—in the words of Augustine of Hippo—in the direction of two extremes antithetical to each other: "*amor sui usque ad contemptum Dei*" on one hand, and "*amor Dei usque ad contemptum sui*"[1] on the other. The latter extreme found its most perfect realization in the Cross of Christ, who "humbled himself and became obedient to the point of death" (Phil 2:8).

Christ's "obedience" "to death" includes *the Son's sovereign act of the will* (cf. Jn 10:15–18); it is an act of love greater than all the evil of which the free will of creatures is capable. Even the most unbridled "*amor sui usque ad contemptum Dei*" remains disproportionately surpassed by this sacrificial act of Christ's love. On the wood of the Cross, Jesus *reveals the love capable of "fulfilling all justice."* This is the love of the Son of Man—truly human—and at the same time it is the love that has a dimension proper to God: the Son, consubstantial with the Father, accomplishes this act of saving love in the Trinitarian "Communion." The Son is at the same time "the firstborn of all creation" (Col 1:15), and he is the Word through whom "all things came into being" (Jn 1:3).

6. The reality of the redemption of the world belongs to the earthly history of humankind and at the same time constitutes the ineffable *mystery of the inner Life of God*. Christ, on the eve before his Passion, said to the apostles: "It is to your advantage that I go away, for if I do not go away, the Advocate will not come to you; but if I go, I will send him to you" (Jn 16:7). Thus, the power of Christ's "departure" on the Cross *takes on a new beginning, the "sharing"* of the Holy Spirit with the world, and in particular with humankind. This "sharing" of God *is saving by nature*. The world, and the human being in the world, cannot be saved in any other way than by transcending himself, his own created "I," toward the Life that comes from God. This Life is a gift similar to the life-giving water that, thanks to the Holy Spirit, will become in the person "a spring of water gushing up to eternal life" (Jn 4:14).

7. Redemption is the reconciliation of justice with love, in which *love* is revealed to be "the greatest." *Beyond all the dimensions of evil, sin, and death,* in which humankind has become entangled by primordial "disobedience," *the crucified and risen Christ manifests the freedom of God, in which immutably remains the will to salvation*. The Paschal Mystery of Jesus Christ, and in particular his Resurrection on "the third day," is the "confirmation" of this saving will "for all" (cf. Acts 17:30–31).

8. When the Apostle *Paul of Tarsus* sees the altar *in Athens* with the inscription "To an unknown god," the perspective of the mystery that has profoundly changed his life opens up before him. The "unknown God" is precisely the one whom Paul had been given to know outside the walls of the city of Damascus: "I am Jesus, whom you are persecuting" (cf. Acts 9:5). But is this only an invisible "unknown God," absolutely transcendent with respect to the world? *Or is it perhaps even more astonishing that this God,* who in himself is a Trinitarian Communion, has accomplished the salvation of the world in his eternal Son "born of a woman" (cf. Gal 4:4)? And that "taking the form of a servant" has redeemed humanity on the wood of a cross? *At the price of his own blood?*

Paul was given the knowledge of this truth about God; it was given to him "to bring to the Gentiles the news of the boundless riches of Christ" (Eph 3:8). "What therefore you worship as unknown, this I proclaim to you": *the God in whom "we live and move and have our being"* (Acts 17:28). But is this just an almighty Creator? The "ONE who IS"? Or maybe further: a Redeemer? The One who has overcome everything? And creates all things anew? The ONE who is LOVE?

Notes

"*Dulcis . . .*" is from the Pentecost Sunday Gospel Sequence *Veni, Sancte Spiritus.*

1. Latin, "love of self to the point of indifference toward God" and "love of God to the point of indifference toward self" (Augustine of Hippo, *De Civitate Dei*, 14, 28: CSEL 40, 2, 56).

VIII.

CHRIST "REVEALS MAN TO HIMSELF"

Tuorum fidelium
Sine Tuo numine
nihil est in homine
nihil est innoxium
Lava quod est sordidum
riga quod est aridum

Where you are not, we have naught,
Nothing good in deed or thought,
Nothing free from taint of ill.
Heal our wounds, our strength renew;
On our dryness pour your dew.

1. *"For we too are his offspring"* (Acts 17:28). The apostle at the Areopagus quotes the words of the Greek poets. At the same time, his thoughts are directed to God who, in the Resurrection of Christ, has given "assurance to all" of his eternal will to save the world. This is why the one who "rose from the dead" had the name Jesus, a name that means "God who saves." To save us, God, who is absolutely transcendent with respect to the world, has worked in the world, at the center of human history, in the "fullness of time" (Gal 4:4). The saving action of God—the *mystery of Redemption*—was the subject of the previous catechesis. Today we must *contemplate this same mystery further, from the human perspective.* It is precisely thanks to the mystery of the Redemption that the words of Paul at the Areopagus find confirmation—a radical confirmation: "We too are his offspring."

2. The Second Vatican Council expresses this truth in the Constitution *Gaudium et Spes*: "The truth is that only in the mystery of the incarnate Word does the mystery of man take on light. For Adam, the first man, was a figure of Him Who was to come (Rom 5:14), namely Christ the Lord. *Christ*, the final Adam, by the revelation of the mystery of the Father and His love, *fully reveals man to man himself and makes his supreme calling clear*" (GS, 22).

The key lies in this phrase: Christ fully reveals man to himself! This statement can provoke astonishment and also awaken resistance and opposition, especially for the contemporary critical mentality that is increasingly positivistic. Is man not already sufficiently known, thanks to the vast research in the most varied scientific disciplines? Isn't man already fully known and explored by his own reason? So how can we talk about the "revelation" of man?

But . . . just as among the many Athenian altars dedicated to the gods of the Greek Olympus, there is an altar with the dedication "To an unknown god," so among the many works written about humankind in the twentieth century, we find one entitled *Man, the Unknown*,[1] whose author is not a theologian but a scientist.

3. What does it mean that Christ "reveals man to himself" and that he "fully reveals" him? The council responds to this question in a convincing way. *First of all, Christ himself is truly human*: "He worked with human hands, He thought with a human mind, acted by human choice. . . . Born of the Virgin Mary, He has truly been made one of us, like us in all things except sin (cf. Heb 4:15)" (*GS*, 22).

By his holiness, "He . . . is Himself the perfect man"; in fact, the whole of the New Testament testifies that "by His incarnation the Son of God has united Himself in some fashion with every man" (*GS*, 22).

This humanity of his, united in one Person with the divine nature of God the Son, attests to the incomparable exaltation of humanity. Humankind must have an extraordinary value in the eyes of God, if for his salvation the very Son of God became human. "Each of us" can repeat in full faith with the apostle: *the Son of God has "loved me and gave himself for me"* (Gal 2:20). These words refer to the sacrifice of Christ on the Cross.

4. At this point, we touch on a question that has always tormented the human race—the question in which every human person has his particular "particle." It is *the problem of suffering* and, more generally, *of evil in the world* in which we live. This problem raises the fundamental questions that the person addresses to God as creator. These questions are continually expressed in human history, in the context of various cultures and religions. Some of them, such as Buddhism, try to show the human being how to liberate himself from the evil of earthly existence. On the other hand, it must be said that the *Holy Bible* is also *a great book about suffering*. In the Old Testament the righteous Job never stops lamenting, just to mention the most eloquent and moving voice; but there are many other voices like this in the Bible. The New Testament contains above all the message of salvation in Jesus Christ, but *the price of this redemption, of this salvation, is suffering: the mystery of the Cross of Christ.*

5. The council teaches: "As an innocent lamb He merited for us life by the free shedding of His own blood. In Him God reconciled us to Himself and among ourselves; from bondage to the devil and sin He delivered us" (*GS*, 22). "Through Christ and in Christ, the riddles of sorrow and death grow meaningful. Apart from His Gospel, they overwhelm us. Christ has risen, destroying death by His death; He has lavished life upon us so that, as sons in the Son, we can cry out in the Spirit; Abba, Father!" (*GS*, 22) (cf. Acts 8:15; Gal 4:6; Jn 1:12; 1 Jn 3:1–2).

The human question regarding evil in the world, the aspiration to free ourselves from the suffering of human existence, is found at the very center of the Gospel. And there, one always finds an answer to this question. The council recalls: "Pressing upon the Christian to be sure, are the need and the duty to battle against evil through manifold tribulations and even to suffer death. But, linked with the Paschal Mystery and patterned on the dying Christ, he will hasten forward to resurrection in the strength which comes from hope" (*GS*, 22).

6. The Cross and the Resurrection—the Paschal Mystery—constitute the deepest dimension of God's self-revelation in Christ. At the same time and in the same dimension there is also the "revelation of man to man himself" of which the council speaks. During the fulfillment of his messianic mission on earth, Christ repeatedly addressed people with a call: "Come," "Follow me" (cf. Mt 4:19, 8:22, 10:38, 11:28–29; Mk 1:17; Lk 5:10). In this way he indicated that his human existence is the foundation for every human being to resolve questions about the meaning of his own existence and the direction of his calling. In Christ, this sense, as well as the truth about the human person and his dignity, "find their root" and at the same time "attain their crown" (cf. *GS*, 22).

7. The *contemporary person*, especially in the context of Western civilization, *sees freedom as his very reason for being*. His goal for human existence is to achieve maximum autonomy. However, this person cannot fail to perceive that

Christ is the embodiment of perfect freedom. A significant thing: the one who repeatedly submits to the will of the Father, always wanting to carry it out, shows us at the same time that he acts in an autonomous and sovereign way. However, this *perfect freedom of the Son of man is always a freedom of commitment.* Christ lives "for the Father"—but is also "a man for others" in the most authentic sense of the word. "The Son of Man came not to be served but to serve, and to give his life a ransom for many" (Mt 20:28). This is the absolute confirmation of the fact that "to reign" means "to serve."

8. "Indeed, the Lord Jesus, when He prayed to the Father, 'that all may be one . . . as we are one' (Jn 17:21–22) opened up vistas closed to human reason, for he implied a certain likeness between the union of the divine Persons and the unity of God's children in truth and charity. This likeness reveals that *the human being,* who is the only creature on earth which God willed for itself, *cannot fully find himself except through a sincere gift of himself*" (GS, 24).

Thus Christ confirms the truth about freedom, by which the human person is an individual and sovereign being. At the same time, however, he indicates with power and determination that in this human freedom (in the likeness of God's freedom) is inscribed the "necessity" of gift. In this sense, Christ is the "gospel of freedom," the "sincere gift of self" that testifies to the fact that the human being is "God's offspring."

It is necessary that *this truth be taken into careful consideration by contemporary* advocates and supporters of an anthropology that considers the human being as "absolute freedom" on earth. According to them, only freedom in itself is a value and a goal.

NOTES

"*Tuorum . . .*" is from the Pentecost Sunday Gospel Sequence, *Veni, Sancte Spiritus.*

1. Alexis Carrel, *Man the Unknown* (New York: Harper & Brothers, 1935); original edition, *L'homme cet inconnu* (Paris: Plon, 1935). Alexis Carrel (1873–1944), French physiologist and surgeon, was a professor at the Rockefeller Institute in New York, where for thirty-two years he taught biology and researched organ transplantation, animal tissue culture, and blood vessel suture. For this work, he was awarded the Nobel Prize in 1912.

IX.

THE EUCHARIST AND THE CHURCH

Sana quod est saucium
Flecte quod est rigidum
Fove quod est frigidum
Rege quod est devium
Da tuis fidelibus
in te confidentibus

Wash the stains of guilt away:
Bend the stubborn heart and will;
Melt the frozen, warm the chill;
Guide the steps that go astray.
On the faithful, who adore
And confess you, evermore.

1. At the Areopagus, Paul of Tarsus announces the risen Christ. He proclaims that truth about the "unknown God" which was confirmed to the apostles by Jesus in the evening "of that first day of the week" when he entered the Cenacle through the closed door and said to them: "As the Father has sent me, so I send you. . . . Receive the Holy Spirit" (Jn 20:19–22). This happened on the third day after Jesus' Crucifixion, after his death on Golgotha, and his burial in the tomb. Appearing in the Cenacle, Christ showed the apostles the wounds on his hands and feet pierced by nails, and his side which the centurion had pierced with the spear to confirm his death. The apostles were in the Upper Room behind closed doors. They were still terrified. Of course, Paul was not with them then; but the words of Christ were for him also, by virtue of the particular calling he would receive later.

2. The *Cenacle of Jerusalem*: the place of the most sacred encounters; the place of the most important institutions. This is where all that we Christians live, from generation to generation, began. On Easter evening, Jesus returned to that same Cenacle where a few days earlier, on Thursday, *during the Passover supper*, he had said goodbye to the apostles before the Passion. He had told them: "It is to your advantage that I go away, for if I do not go away, the Advocate will not come to you; but if I go, I will send him to you" (Jn 16:7). He spoke of the Holy Spirit that they would receive by virtue of his redeeming death on the Cross. He had also said: *"I am going away, and I am coming to you"* (Jn 14:28). Then he added: "Your pain will turn into joy" (Jn 16:20). All

this was fulfilled on the evening "after the sabbath." Here, it seemed he was irrevocably "gone" (no one, after all, returns from beyond the boundaries of death). But instead he has "come," and the disciples "rejoiced when they saw the Lord" (Jn 20:20).

Entering, "he breathed on them" and said, "Receive the Holy Spirit." He "gave" them the promised Spirit, the Comforter; he entrusted it to them, one could say, in the signs of his redemptive Passion and his death on the Cross. He stood before them as "the last Adam" who became a "life-giving spirit" (1 Cor 15:45).

3. *In the power of this Spirit the memory of the Last Supper* that Christ shared with them in that same Cenacle, on the eve of his Passion, *is revived in the minds of the apostles.* They all remember how during that dinner, following the ancient rite of the Jewish Passover, he took bread, broke it, and gave it to them, saying: "Take, all of you, and eat it: this is my Body which is given for you." Then he took the cup filled with wine and gave it to them, saying: "Take, all of you, and drink from it: this is *the cup of my Blood for the new and eternal covenant, which is poured out for you and for many* (all) *for the forgiveness of sins.*" Finally he added: "Do this in memory of me" (cf. Mt 26:26–28; Mk 14:22–24; Lk 22:17–20; 1 Cor 11:23–25).

4. Was it only about preserving the memory of the last Passover meal? The words that Jesus spoke about bread and wine clearly show that this was not just a supper. Jesus explicitly speaks of his body offered as a sacrifice (and he

says it while giving bread to his disciples), and speaks (over the cup) of the blood shed for the remission of sins that becomes the Blood of the Covenant—New and Eternal—between God and humankind. With this Blood, *"with his own blood,"* Christ *"entered once for all into the Holy Place . . . thus obtaining eternal redemption"* (cf. Heb 9:12). He enters as the one priest of the whole history of humanity and of the world, as "high priest of the good things that have come" (cf. Heb 9:11): the only "mediator between God and humankind" (cf. 1 Tm 2:5); the redeemer of all and of every one. In this way "God so loved the world."

And at the same time, *that same body* offered in sacrifice on the Cross and *that same blood* shed for the remission of sins *remain under the species of Bread and Wine the Sacrament* instituted at the Last Supper, the sacrament entrusted to the apostles and to the Church: "Do this." Entrusted for all time, until the final coming of the Risen Lord.

5. "Receive the Holy Spirit. . . ." In the power of this Spirit, Christ returning to the Father remains with his disciples and with the Church: "I am going away and I am coming to you." In a special way he remains in the sacrament of his redeeming sacrifice which is given for the nourishment of the People of the New Covenant on their journey toward the "Father's house" (cf. *LG*, 3).

"Do not work for the food that perishes, but for the food that endures for eternal life, which the Son of Man will give you" (Jn 6:27)—so Jesus said when the crowd sought him out to proclaim him king after the miracle of the multiplication of the loaves. And he added:

"For the bread of God is that which comes down
from heaven and gives life to the world."

"Sir, give us this bread always."

"I am the bread of life. Whoever comes to me
will never be hungry, and whoever believes in me
will never be thirsty." (Jn 6:33–35)

6. This announcement (written in the sixth chapter of John's
gospel) was the preamble to what would happen at the Last
Supper. The crowd at Capernaum *could not understand how
Jesus* of Nazareth (many of them had known him personally
for a long time) *could be "the bread that comes down from
heaven."* Against their doubts and even their opposition
(because many had since stopped listening to the Teacher
from Nazareth), Christ confirmed even more clearly what
from the day of Holy Thursday remains the eucharistic mystery of the Church. He said:

> I am the living bread that came down from heav-
> en; *whoever eats of this bread will live forever*; and
> the bread that I will give for the life of the world
> is my flesh. . . . Unless you eat the flesh of the Son
> of Man and drink his blood, you have no life in
> you. Those who eat my flesh and drink my blood
> have eternal life, and I will raise them up on the
> last day; for *my flesh is true food, and my blood
> is true drink.* Those who eat my flesh and drink
> my blood abide in me, and I in them. Just as the
> living Father sent me, and I live because of the
> Father, so whoever eats me will live because of
> me. (Jn 6:51–57)

7. The apostles gathered in the Cenacle for the Passover meal with their Master; they remember that his words at Capernaum were a "difficult teaching" for many and how Christ had asked them if they too wanted to leave him. There, Peter replied: *"Lord, to whom can we go? You have the words of eternal life"* (Jn 6:68).

Here the "words of eternal life" previously heard are restated in the form of the eucharistic institution: "Take and eat. . . . This is my Body. . . . Take and drink. . . . This is the cup of my Blood."

At the end of his discourse at Capernaum, Jesus added: "It is the spirit that gives life; the flesh is useless. The words that I have spoken to you are spirit and life" (cf. Jn 6:63).

Christ's words of the institution in the Upper Room are open to the Spirit who gives life. The Eucharist as a sacrament of the Body and Blood of the Lord, as a sacrament of the redemption of the world, awaits the coming of the Holy Spirit. "Receive the Holy Spirit," Jesus says to the apostles after the Resurrection. He says it in that same Cenacle in which he had instituted the Sacrament of his Body and Blood "for the life of the world." In this way *Christ anticipates what on the day of Pentecost will become reality.*

8. The apostles will await this day in the Cenacle, gathered in prayer with Mary, the Mother of the Lord. In this expectation, a double consciousness accompanies them: *consciousness of the institution made at the Last Supper* when Jesus commanded them: "Do this in memory of me"; and *consciousness of the mission* he had entrusted to them as he returned to the Father: "Go therefore and make disciples of

all nations, baptizing them in the name of the Father and of the Son and of the Holy Spirit, and teaching them to obey everything that I have commanded you" (Mt 28:19–20).

On the day of Pentecost this consciousness, which until then had been accompanied by a sense of weakness and fear, suddenly changed into "power from on high." They were "baptized in the Holy Spirit." From this baptism they emerged mature, as though born again. To the representatives of the various nations "under heaven" who gathered in Jerusalem (on the occasion of the feast), they began to preach about "God's deeds of power" in different languages (cf. Acts 2:5–11).

Not only were the apostles born to new life. The Church, too, was born to its universal mission and destiny. At that moment *the Church*, like a newborn coming out of the mother's womb, *appeared in the world*. Christ formed it once and for all, with his Body and Blood offered "for the life of the world" (cf. Jn 6:51). "The spirit that gives life" constantly causes everyone who "feeds on Christ" in the Eucharist to have life because of him, just as Christ has life "because of the Father" (cf. Jn 6:57).

NOTES

"*Sana . . .*" is from the Pentecost Sunday Gospel Sequence, *Veni, Sancte Spiritus*.

X.

"RECEIVE THE HOLY SPIRIT"

Sacrum Septenarium
Da virtutis meritum
Da salutis exitum
Da perenne Gaudium

Amen
Alleluia

In your sevenfold gift descend;
Give them virtue's sure reward;
Give them your salvation, Lord;
Give them joys that never end.

Amen. Alleluia.

1. In the present series of catecheses, we refer to the Acts of the Apostles. The point of reference is the event at the Areopagus of Athens, not only Paul's discourse, but the entirety of this significant event. One can say that it is one of *the milestones in the journey of the Church*, precisely at the beginning of her history. A dozen or so years earlier, this apostolic Church had left the Cenacle of Jerusalem on the day of Pentecost. On that day the Church appeared to the world in her full identity. She was revealed as God's "New Covenant" with humankind in the crucified and risen Christ: a Covenant being fulfilled in the power of the Holy Spirit. Peter's words on the day of Pentecost testify that the apostles, "baptized in the Holy Spirit," *became witnesses of Christ and his Gospel in the world.* Christ sent them to proclaim him not only in Jerusalem, in Judea, and in Samaria, but "to the ends of the earth."

2. And here we are together with *Paul at the Areopagus of Athens.* On that day, when the apostle tried to bring his listeners closer to the truth about the "unknown God," to the God they "worship without knowing," it would have been impossible to foresee the consequences of that (apparently failed) encounter. These would only manifest themselves later in the gradual development of events. If we now refer to that moment in the Acts of the Apostles, as has been said before, we do it from the perspective of our era and its specific problems. They seem to be two very distant worlds. *The world at the end of the second millennium after Christ* is completely different from the ancient one, and in many respects incomparable. How much more penetrated by

the ingenuity of the human mind, how much more "subordinated" and mastered by humankind in various fields, conquered and appropriated by all that humankind has achieved in the field of science, technology, and civilization!

3. Here we should refer to the Second Vatican Council, and in particular to the Pastoral Constitution *Gaudium et Spes*. At the beginning of this document there is a *summary of "the situation of men in the modern world."* This summary speaks to the conditions of human existence that have undergone many changes, and it frames these changes in the social, psychological, moral, as well as religious spheres, taking into consideration the "inequalities, contradictions, and imbalances" characteristic of our age (cf. *GS*, 8).

Undoubtedly, "the conviction grows not only that humanity can and should increasingly consolidate its control over creation, but even more, that it devolves on humanity to establish a political, social and economic order which will growingly serve man and help individuals as well as groups to affirm and develop the dignity proper to them" (*GS*, 9).

4. Typical of the contemporary world are *multiple "demands."* "Beneath all these demands lies," according to the council, "a deeper and more widespread longing: persons and societies thirst for a full and free life worthy of man; one in which they can subject to their own welfare all that the modern world can offer them so abundantly" (*GS*, 9). *The council confronts* these "demands," which are just in themselves, in a realistic way *with the "imbalances under*

which the modern world labors." These "are linked with that more basic imbalance which is rooted in the heart of man": *within the human being.* "He suffers from internal divisions, and from these flow so many and such great discords in society" (*GS*, 10). "Since all these things are so, the modern world shows itself at once *powerful* and *weak, capable of the noblest deeds or the foulest.*" The task of the human being is "to guide aright the forces which he has unleashed and which can enslave him or minister to him" (*GS*, 9).

5. The council observes the situation of the world from the human perspective: the multiple "imbalances under which the modern world labors." The council looks through the *inner contradiction that is in humankind.* From the beginning, the world was "subjected" and entrusted to humankind; therefore the human being shapes this "world" according to his abilities, his genius, but also on the basis of that contradiction that is within him. What the Bible calls the *"sin of the world"* accompanies human history from the beginning. It has put its roots into the human being and from him it spreads ever further.

   "The Church firmly believes that Christ, who died and was raised up for all, can through His Spirit offer man the light and the strength to measure up to his supreme destiny" (*GS*, 10). In the teaching of Vatican II, we find at every step expressions that bear witness to this faith: "The world . . . created and sustained by its Maker's love, [is] fallen indeed into the bondage of sin, yet emancipated now by Christ, Who was crucified and rose again to break the strangle hold of personified evil, so that the world might be fashioned

anew according to God's design and reach its fulfillment" (*GS*, 2).

6. What the Church of our time affirms through the council constitutes *the Church's message of faith since the day of Pentecost in Jerusalem.* Peter was the first to proclaim this faith on behalf of all the apostles gathered in the Cenacle. This same truth was announced by Paul of Tarsus at the Athenian Areopagus, taking into account the mentality of those who listened to him there. Although the ways of bearing witness to Christ in Peter's *kerygma* in Jerusalem and Paul's in Athens are different, the substance of the content remains the same, as does their objective: "repent—*metanoeite*" (cf. Acts 17:30).

To *"repent" means: to enter into the life-giving mystery of Christ!* Draw from it! In him "God so loved the world" (Jn 3:16). "God did not send the Son into the world to condemn the world, but in order that the world might be saved through him" (Jn 3:17). To save the world, to redeem humankind, *Christ takes upon himself in the sacrifice of the Cross "the sin of the world"* that weighs on the history of humanity. He takes sin, going back to its primordial dimension in the mystery of human origins. He conquers the evil of sin, by "becoming sin for our sake" (cf. 2 Cor 5:21) just as he overcomes death with his own death.

The first words that Jesus speaks to the apostles after the Resurrection confirm this: *"Receive the Holy Spirit. If you forgive the sins of any,* they are forgiven them" (Jn 20:22–23).

7. It should be added that the apostle Paul, in a particularly penetrating way, revealed and expressed the truth about that firstfruit of the redeeming Death and Resurrection of Christ that is linked to the *sacrament of Baptism*. He writes in the Letter to the Romans: "Do you not know that all of us who have been baptized into Christ Jesus were baptized into his death? Therefore we have been buried with him by baptism into death, so that, just as Christ was raised from the dead by the glory of the Father, so we too might walk in newness of life. . . . We know that *our old self was crucified with him* so that the body of sin might be destroyed, and we might no longer be enslaved to sin. . . . But if we have died with Christ, we believe that *we will also live with him*" (Rom 6:3–8).

Christ himself once announced to Nicodemus a new birth from water and the Holy Spirit. After his Resurrection, he instructed the apostles and the Church to go among the nations of the world, baptizing them in the name of the Father and of the Son and of the Holy Spirit (cf. Mt 28:19).

To this day, Baptism—the sacrament of saving initiation—remains *the basic element of the unity* among all Christians, despite historical divisions.

8. "The Church firmly believes that Christ, who died and was raised up for all, can through His Spirit offer man the light and the strength to measure up to his supreme destiny" (*GS*, 10). The Church accomplishes this in a sacramental way through Baptism. At the same time, however, she believes that *the divine economy of salvation and grace extends beyond the limits of the Church's sacramental action.*

Christ died for everyone, and is risen. Everyone has been redeemed by his sacrifice on the Cross, even those who are not aware of it. Because the Holy Spirit "blows where it chooses" (cf. Jn 3:8).

No one else, only he, the Spirit of Truth, in the power of Christ's redemption, can *touch that profound discrepancy* that is within the human being, that brokenness that is in him. This testifies that the human being participates in the "sin of the world" and that he contributes to producing it.

The Church believes that *greater* than this evil, greater than the "sin of the world," is love. Above all things is the love with which God loved the world: he loved it in his Only-begotten Son, whom he "gave" for the redemption of the world. This love "has been poured into our hearts through the Holy Spirit that has been given to us" (Rom 5:5).

NOTES

"*Sacrum . . .*" is from the Pentecost Sunday Gospel Sequence, *Veni, Sancte Spiritus.*

XI.

"YOU WILL BE MY WITNESSES"

Adoro te devote
Latens Deitas
quae sub his figuris
vere latitas
Tibi se cor meum totum subjicit,
Quia, te contemplans

I devoutly adore you,
hidden God,
beneath these appearances
truly hidden:
my whole heart submits to you,
and in contemplating you.

1. *"What therefore you worship as unknown, this I proclaim to you"* (Acts 17:23). The words spoken by the apostle at the Areopagus are addressed to a specific audience. But at the same time, these words have a wide range of action and a far-reaching resonance. Paul of Tarsus proclaims a God who revealed himself in Jesus Christ. Christ is the eternal Word of God, the Son consubstantial with the Father, the witness of the Trinitarian mystery. And at the same time, he is the Son of Man, truly human, born of the Virgin Mary in the "fullness of time" (cf. Gal 4:4). *Paul of Tarsus is the apostle of the crucified and risen Christ.* He preaches in Athens and in all the places of his tireless apostolic journeys throughout the world of that time. In Christ, the "unknown God" makes himself known to humanity. The Athenians, by worshipping the "unknown God," turn—according to the apostle—not to someone else, but to the One whom he himself proclaims: to the God who revealed himself in the crucified and risen Christ.

2. Nearly two thousand years have passed since the Athenian event. From generation to generation, *the Church proclaims to humanity Jesus Christ, who "is the same yesterday and today and forever"* (Heb 13:8). The message of the Church continuously reaches new people. Yet the total number of Christians does not exceed 30 percent of the current inhabitants of our planet earth.[1] Thus, the inscription on the Athenian altar "To an unknown god" is still valid, just as the words of Paul continue to be relevant today regarding the One whom humanity—for the most

part—"worships as unknown." There are various reasons for this state of affairs.

3. The Second Vatican Council states that "those who have not yet received the Gospel are related in various ways to the people of God" (*LG*, 16). Here, the Church looks, first of all, to the people of the Old Covenant, but also to the followers of Islam who, evoking Abraham's faith, "along with us adore the one and merciful God, who on the last day will judge mankind" (*LG*, 16). Belonging to the People of God, according to the teaching of the Second Vatican Council, extends even further and involves ever wider circles. This "unknown God" of the Pauline sermon at the Areopagus is not only the Creator of all things. He also "desires everyone to be saved and to come to the knowledge of the truth" (1 Tm 2:4). Christ, who redeemed all, is an expression of the Father's saving will.

Also included as the people of God are *"those . . . who through no fault of their own do not know the Gospel of Christ or His Church*, yet *sincerely seek God* and moved by grace strive by their deeds to do His will" (*LG*, 16). And also "those who, without blame on their part, have not yet arrived at an explicit knowledge of God and with His grace *strive to live a good life*" (the council adds that this, however, is not possible "without divine grace") (see *LG*, 16).

4. So how far does the circle of those of whom the apostle at the Areopagus says "worship as unknown" (the true God) extend? It is difficult to answer this question based on human calculations and statistics. The answer is *known to*

God alone. Conclusions must be drawn from what the last council teaches about belonging to the Church and "assignment" to the People of God.

5. But even more strongly the call of the apostle thunders: "Woe to me if I do not proclaim the gospel!" (1 Cor 9:16). Since God revealed himself, in his ineffable mystery, in Jesus Christ, and Jesus Christ entrusted this mystery to the apostles and to the Church, the imperative to proclaim the Gospel to every creature resounds unceasingly: to those to whom the Gospel still is not known, to those who know it insufficiently or do not put it into practice enough, and finally to those who know it but, for various reasons, ignore it. Perhaps it would be necessary in many places of the contemporary world to construct an altar not so much to the "God unknown," *but to the "God ignored."*

6. "What therefore you worship as unknown, this I proclaim to you." The Apostle of Tarsus, and with him the whole Church, from generation to generation, proclaims Christ. He himself said: "Whoever has seen me has seen the Father" (Jn 14:9). And so *the Church proclaims Christ to make the Father better known.* And at the same time, it proclaims Christ, because *in him the mystery of humankind is fully manifested.* Christ "fully reveals man to man himself" (*GS,* 22). These two dimensions of the gospel message are closely linked. In Christ, the human being "sees the Father," and at the same time in Christ the human being meets himself; he discovers the depth of his humanity, and also the full

meaning of his existence and calling, which is inscribed in the very fact of being human.

The time in which Jesus of Nazareth carried out his messianic mission was brief. Those who heard and watched him, and especially those who were with him as disciples and apostles, *learned from Christ anew what it means to be human*. This experience reached the peak of its maturity on the day of Pentecost. From the coming of the Paraclete, from the moment in which they were "baptized in the Holy Spirit," the proclamation of Christ was fulfilled in them: "You will be my witnesses" (Acts 1:8). This proclamation was then fulfilled for generations and generations in all those who "through the word of the Apostles believed in Christ" (cf. Jn 17:20; Acts 4:4, 15:7).

7. *What does it mean "to be witnesses"?* What does it mean to "give testimony"? It means: uniting oneself to Christ to "see the Father" (cf. Jn 14:9) in him and through him. But at the same time, "to be a witness" and "to give testimony" means "to *read in Christ* the mystery of man." It means "to be human": to read in him *the meaning and sense of his own humanity*, "to draw from him" under the action of the Spirit of Truth, which in turn continually "draws" from him (cf. Jn 16:13–15). Christ in his unique and unrepeatable humanity is a gift for all. He is not only the "mirror" in which the human being can see deified humanity but also *a gift that deifies the humanity of those who welcome him*. In this way, by virtue of the Holy Spirit, we become "sons in the Son."

8. Therefore, "being a witness" of Christ means "drawing from his fullness"; somehow entering into that Divinity-Humanity that along with him has become "the way and the truth and the life" (cf. Jn 14:6) of human history, and *from him to discover a new maturity of one's own humanity, of one's own person*. In this process of transformation the person does not lose himself, his humanity, or his proper dimension; on the contrary: he finds this humanity and its right dimension. Is not the measure of humanity really "the image and likeness" of God himself?

Christ, once for all and for everyone, has become a "cornerstone" of the actual realization of this fundamental dimension of humanity through the Spirit of Truth.

9. When asked, "Teacher, what good deed must I do to have eternal life?" he replied, *"Keep the commandments."* In fact, the proper dimension of humanity is the moral good, virtue (as the antithesis of evil, of sin). To the question: "What do I still lack?" he replied, "Follow me" (cf. Mt 19:21). This evangelical response, both the first and the second, is always highly relevant. It has universal validity. It is supra-temporal and at the same time concrete. Everyone, guided by conscience, can apply it to himself. People of all ages, education, status, and profession can do it. It speaks to young people and mature adults, as well as to people marked by life, the elderly, and the sick.

In this response, *Christ* "reveals man to himself" or rather *confirms humanity through the moral virtue* that is fundamental for every individual. Christ's message to the world embraces all that is humanly true, good, and beautiful. It refers to all areas of human morality and human creativity.

10. The answer, however, is not limited to this dimension alone. When Christ says to the apostles and consequently to all his other disciples from generation to generation: "you will be my witnesses" (cf. Acts 1:8), he indicates another dimension. It is the sacramental dimension through which Christ himself acts in a human being who opens himself to his action in the power of the Spirit of Truth.

"Since the Church is in Christ like a sacrament . . . of a very closely knit union with God and of the unity of the whole human race" (*LG*, 1.1), it is in this Church *Christ still works through the sacraments* of our faith: from Baptism to the Sacrament of Confirmation, from the Eucharist to the Sacrament of Reconciliation (or Penance) and to the Anointing of the Sick, through the priesthood and marriage; he always creates the conditions for the human being to learn the fullness of his humanity. At the same time, he creates the conditions for carrying out the apostolic mission: "You will be my witnesses." May this mission be realized in the varied moments of Christian life, in the different contexts and vocations. May it be realized *through the richness and multiplicity of gifts*: "Each one receives from God a gift . . . his own gift" (cf. *LG*, 2, 11–12).

NOTES

"*Adoro* . . .": here Archbishop Wojtyła begins inscribing some lines from the text of *Adoro te devote*, a hymn to the Eucharist written by St. Thomas Aquinas in 1264 for the first Solemnity of Corpus Christi, at the request of Pope Urban IV. It is often sung or recited during the Benediction of the Blessed Sacrament.

1. At the time, nearly 5 billion people.

XII.

LOVE: REDEMPTIVE AND SPOUSAL

totum deficit
Visus, tactus, gustus
in Te fallitur
sed auditu solo
tuto creditur

It surrenders itself completely.
Sight, touch, taste
are all deceived in their judgment of you,
but hearing alone suffices
firmly to believe.

1. *"Woe to me if I do not proclaim the Gospel!"* (1 Cor 9:16). These words express *the apostle's interior imperative.* This imperative brought Paul of Tarsus to the roads of the world of that time. It also brought him to Athens, to the Areopagus. It compelled him to preach the crucified and risen Christ to those for whom this truth was distant and foreign: "a sign of contradiction."[1] However, the apostle was not discouraged. He, as well as all those who were given "to suffer dishonor for the sake of the name" of Jesus (cf. Acts 5:41), have not ceased to proclaim this name, deeply convinced that "we must obey God rather than any human authority" (Acts 5:29). From this heroic "obedience of faith" was born the imperative of evangelization, which proved to be even more powerful than bloody persecution, especially in the first three centuries under the Roman Empire, and later in different centuries and various places of the Ecumene (*oikoumene*, "the house where we all live").

2. *In this way the Church*, of which Christ himself spoke in many parables, *propagated itself.* In this Church, Christ dwells as the One through whom the Father "loved the world." For her too he "prepared a Kingdom," his Kingdom which is the eschatological fulfillment of history. Christ, sending the apostles, said: *"And I confer on you, just as my Father has conferred on me, a kingdom"* (Lk 22:29). From then on, in the history of the world the eschatological "leaven" works and the "growth" of this kingdom, which is the ultimate goal and destiny of all creation, is accomplished. The kingdom's "growth" will come to its fullness *when God will "be all in all"* (cf. 1 Cor 15:28). This will

be accomplished through Christ when he "hands over the kingdom to God the Father" (cf. 1 Cor 15:24–28) as the ripe fruit of the Redemption. Then he who is "the First"—"the firstborn of all creation" (Col 1:15)—will manifest himself as "the Last"—"the Alpha and the Omega" of all things (cf. Rv 1:8, 21:6, 22:13).

3. The Kingdom of God is "*already*" in the world, in the history of humanity, but "*not yet*" in its proper dimension. The Church that prays every day: "Thy kingdom come" sees in the fulfillment of this prayer her fundamental mission.

Fully aware of human sinfulness—of the people who, thanks to the redemption of Christ, have become the true People of God, *the Church firmly believes* and trusts. *Indeed, Christ loved the Church* just as, in the Old Covenant, YHWH loved Israel; and no infidelity of the Chosen People, no measure of human sin, could change this love.

4. This love of God-YHWH was in a sense a preparation for the love with which Christ loved the Church and never ceases to love her. "Christ loved the church and *gave himself up for her*" (as we read in the Letter to the Ephesians 5:25). This love has a redemptive character: he "gave himself up" in the sense that he "sacrificed himself," and this extreme sacrifice was the "price" of love; it was its immense and indestructible measure. One reads in that same letter that Christ "gave himself up for her" (for the Church), to make her holy, purifying her with the washing of water through the word (referring to the Sacrament of Baptism, in which Christ begins his action in humankind through the sacrament of

water and the Spirit; see Jn 3:5). *This "washing-cleansing" of salvation* must gradually lead to the moment in which Christ will present her "in splendor, without a spot or wrinkle or anything of the kind—yes, so that she may be holy and without blemish" (Eph 5:25–27).

In this way *Christ's love* for the Church—and in the Church for every human being—*takes on a spousal meaning.* It is redemptive and spousal at the same time. "Christ loved the Church" and loves her (and everyone in her) with the love with which a bridegroom loves his bride, and the husband his wife. Spousal love is love wherein *the person* becomes *a gift to a person.*

5. From this love of Christ, which is at the same time redemptive and spousal, originates the sacrament by which man and woman make a gift of themselves to one another and are united in marriage. This unity is inscribed in the very mystery of human creation: "God created humankind in his image; in the image of God he created them; male and female he created them" (Gn 1:27). "Therefore a man leaves his father and his mother and clings to his wife, and *they become one flesh*" (Gn 2:24; cf. Eph 5:31). This special bond has a spousal character in which a person becomes a gift to a person. It is a mutual gift and *a sacramental bond of an indissoluble character.*

6. We cannot fail to mention here the answer that Christ gave to the Pharisees when they asked him if divorce was possible, citing the Law of Moses: "Is it lawful for a man to divorce his wife for any cause?" He replied: "Have you not

read that the one who made them at the beginning 'made them male and female,' and said, 'For this reason a man shall leave his father and mother and be joined to his wife, and the two shall become one flesh'? So they are no longer two, but one flesh. *Therefore what God has joined together, let no one separate*" (Mt 19:3–6). If Moses introduced "a bill of divorce," he did it "because you were so hard-hearted" answered Jesus, "but from the beginning it was not so" (cf. Mt 19:8).

7. What we read in the Letter to the Ephesians clarifies the truth about human marriage and explains why "from the beginning" means that the bond between man and woman is indissoluble. Indeed, in it is realized love that has a spousal character: *the love in which* a person makes a gift of himself to a person. Precisely and only *on the basis of this mutual gift can man and woman become "one flesh" in marriage*; precisely by the fact that the marriage has an indissoluble character. Only in this way, as indissoluble, can it constitute a solid basis for human procreation and upbringing. Only a lasting union of the spouses determines their mature parenthood. They can then keep their word to the Creator, and "willingly and lovingly accept the children he will want to give them" (cf. the *Roman Ritual of the Sacrament of Marriage*). They can also respond to that fundamental trust that every child places in them, as parents and educators, in a certain sense from the first moment of conception.

This is everything: the whole truth about marriage and the family, inscribed in the mystery of creation itself, finds full *confirmation in the Gospel.* It is confirmed by the words of Christ. At the same time, his love, which is simultaneously redemptive and spousal, is the model and the source of spiritual strength for men and women who in the Sacrament of Marriage receive the blessing of Christ working in the Church, a blessing that sanctifies and, so to speak, "consecrates" their love and their vocation in the Church and in society.

8. Christ reveals the human being to himself. Therefore, everyone should learn from him what it means "to be human"—as stated above. This also applies to spouses, men and women who take part in the "great mystery" proclaimed by the author of the Letter to the Ephesians: "*This is a great mystery,* and I am *applying it to Christ and the church.* Each of you, however, should love his wife as himself" (Eph 5:32–33). "Husbands, *love* your wives, just *as Christ loved* the church and gave himself up for her" (Eph 5:25). "He who loves his wife loves himself" (Eph 5:28). But since it is a matter of mutual love, just as the personal gift that unites husband and wife is mutual, then the apostle exhorts: "Be subject to one another out of reverence for Christ" (Eph 5:21). This reverence is also "the beginning of wisdom." It allows in the mutual relationship, as well as in bodily communion, for the opening of oneself to the action of the Holy Spirit's gifts, especially the gift of respect for what comes from God (*donum pietatis*) which protects in the spouses' hearts the "sacredness" of their bodies and their sex.

9. "Christ loved the church and gave himself up for her" (Eph 5:25). From this love, which is redemptive and at the same time spousal, another spousal human love draws particular vital strength. It is *love that is expressed in the voluntary renunciation of marriage* and family happiness *for Christ as sole Spouse.* "And there are eunuchs who have made themselves eunuchs for the sake of the kingdom of heaven. Let anyone accept this who can" (Mt 19:12). In this spousal love live men and women who, by virtue of religious vows, dedicate themselves completely to Christ; and also those who, when they are ordained priests, commit themselves to a celibate (non-marital) life.

In this way *they testify to that particular spiritual freedom that allows them to be at the service* of everyone on the roads of their vocation (as the apostle writes in the seventh chapter of the First Letter to the Corinthians). In this way they also express the truth of the ultimate vocation of the human being in the kingdom that the Father "conferred on the Son" and in which one "neither marries nor is given in marriage" (cf. Mt 22:30). *The eschatological character of the evangelical vocation of humankind* finds in the testimony of these people—men and women—a particularly eloquent confirmation. The love with which Christ loved the Church, redemptive and spousal love, finds in this way the manifestation of its manifold richness. "Love never ends" (1 Cor 13:8).

Notes

"totum . . ." is from the hymn *Adoro te devote.*

1. About a decade after this manuscript was written, the words "sign of contradiction" became the title of the Lenten spiritual exercises prepared and led by Cardinal Karol Wojtyła for Pope Paul VI at the Vatican, March 5–12, 1976. See Karol Wojtyła (Pope John Paul II), *Sign of Contradiction* (New York: Seabury Press, 1979).

XIII.

THE FULLNESS OF PRAYER

Credo quidquid dixit
Dei Filius
nil hoc verbo
Veritatis verius
In cruce latebat
sola Deitas

I believe everything spoken
by the Son of God:
there is nothing truer than this word of
Truth.
On the cross only the divinity was hidden.

1. At the Areopagus of Athens, Paul's discourse on the crucified and risen Christ was not accepted. "When they heard of the resurrection of the dead, some scoffed; but others said, 'We will hear you again about this.' At that point Paul left them" (Acts 17:32–33). Even if on that occasion only "some of them joined him" (Acts 17:34), the time will come when the truth about Christ will gradually spread to Athens, to Greece, and throughout the Roman Empire. *The time will come when Christ will enter the mind and heart of people and of entire peoples.* The time will come when human lips will reverently *speak his name* and *also the prayer* that he himself taught his disciples: *the prayer to the Father.* In the concise words that billions of people across the globe repeat, the entire Good News has been translated into the language of prayer.

2. The Son, who is the Word, consubstantial with the Father, expresses and announces the full truth of Divine Love, because he alone "knows the Father," just as the Father "knows the Son" (cf. Mt 11:27). As "the firstborn of all creation," the Son is the only Word of the invisible and incomprehensible glory for all creation. This inner glory is the prototype of every prayer, the breath of which permeates the whole world: visible and invisible. The macro and the microcosm participate in it—without words—by the very fact that they exist and develop in the footsteps of Eternal Wisdom. *Christ, as the Son of Man, constitutes the summit and the center of prayer* through which people—in the name of all creation—turn to God. They turn to him even

when he is an "unknown God" to them: when they "worship [him] as unknown" (Acts 17:23).

Christ is the teacher of this prayer, through which "true worshipers" worship the Father "in spirit and in truth." Of this prayer "in spirit and truth," Christ is the primary minister, the only Mediator between God and humankind; and prayer is the principal expression of this mediation which in Christ becomes authentic communion. Through prayer, those who are (adopted) children in the only-begotten Son are united to the Father.

3. *We can say that the entire Gospel is a record of this prayer.* At the same time, the moments that Jesus especially dedicates to prayer stand out in the gospel. These are key moments that are fundamental to his mission. The most important of these remains that *in Gethsemane, in the garden of olives*, before the Passion and the Cross, before what Christ called "his hour."

In this prayer Christ united himself to the Father in a special way, and in a special way drew near to him, entering into the eternal dimension of the redemption of the world. However, it must also be emphasized that in this prayer Christ also drew near to humankind in a special way. The words: "If it is possible, let this cup pass from me" (Mt 26:39; cf. Mk 14:35–36) testify to his participation in the suffering of all people from the beginning to the end of the world. *Christ united to the Father*—"Yet, not my will but yours be done" (Lk 22:42)—is at the same time *united to every human being*, and is in "solidarity" with the destiny of humanity on earth. In this prayer Christ opens, so to speak, a special space in which every person can find himself in the most difficult and crucial moments. The prayer in the garden of olives remains the specific paradigm of the "universalism" of Christ in the history of humankind. We can say that this prayer continues unceasingly, and that the history of humanity, in various dimensions, is always being filled again with its intense substance.

Christ said: "The Father will give you whatever you ask him in my name" (cf. Jn 15:16). *Yet could the prayer in Gethsemane go unheard?*

4. We need to read it in connection with another prayer, one that Christ spoke in the Cenacle, just before going to Gethsemane. At that time, he said: "Father, the hour has come; glorify your Son so that the Son may glorify you, since you have given him authority over all people, *to give eternal life to all whom you have given him.* And this is eternal life, that they may know you, the only true God, and Jesus Christ whom you have sent. I glorified you on earth by finishing the work that you gave me to do. So now, Father, glorify me in your own presence with the glory that I had in your presence before the world existed" (Jn 17:1–5).

"If it is possible, *let this cup pass from me*"—"Glorify me": the series of events that make up the whole Paschal Mystery of Jesus Christ testifies to how the Father listened to the prayer of the Son, and how he fulfilled it.

5. This is the moving prayer of the world's Redeemer for those whom the Father "gave him from the world" (cf. Jn 17:6): "They were yours, and you gave them to me. . . .

Holy Father, protect them in your name. . . . I have given them your word. . . . Sanctify them in the truth; your word is truth. As you have sent me into the world, so I have sent them into the world. And for their sakes *I sanctify myself, so that they also may be sanctified in truth*" (Jn 17:7–19).

Christ and the world, Christ—the Church—the world. These two prayers should be read and pondered together: the prayer in Gethsemane and the prayer in the Cenacle (the high-priestly prayer).

Each of us is called to participate in both of these prayers of Christ, *in order to model on their example the Christian "fullness of prayer."*

6. Christ, referring to the apostles who were with him in the Cenacle, says: "I ask not only on behalf of these, but also on behalf of those who will believe in me through their word, that they may all be one. As you, Father, are in me and I am in you, *may they also be in us*, so that the world may believe that you have sent me . . . and have loved them even as you have loved me. . . . I made your name known to them, and I will make it known, so that the love with which you have loved me may be in them, and I in them" (Jn 17:20–26).

In our time, Christians are called to participate in a particular way in the high-priestly prayer of Jesus, in his request for the unity of the Church.

7. As the prayer of Gethsemane is transfused still into the earthly destiny of man, so by virtue of the prayer of the Cenacle Christ is unceasingly present together with the Father who loved the world. He loved it so much "that he

gave his only Son, so that everyone who believes in him may not perish but may have eternal life" (Jn 3:16). *"Father, I desire that those also, whom you have given me, may be with me where I am,* to see my glory, which you have given me because you loved me before the foundation of the world" (Jn 17:24).

Christ "fully reveals man to man himself and makes his supreme calling clear" (*GS,* 22). There is no other, surer way to accept the Christological revelation of humankind than by participation in the prayer of Christ.

8. *To participate in the prayer of Christ* means to believe that "the sufferings of this present time are not worth comparing with the glory about to be revealed to us"—this is what we read in Paul's Letter to the Romans (Rom 8:18). "Creation was subjected to futility, not of its own will but by the will of the one who subjected it, in hope that the creation itself will be set free from its bondage to decay and will obtain the freedom of the glory of the children of God" (Rom 8:20–21).

In hope . . . ! *Prayer is the expression of this hope.* Here the human being is at the center of creation which "has been groaning in labor pains until now." Here the human persons who possess "the first fruits of the Spirit," groan inwardly with all their being "while we wait for adoption, the redemption of our bodies" (cf. Rom 8:22–23).

9. Are we not here together with Christ in Gethsemane? Here, where the Son of God became a participant in our weaknesses. Here, where he received the cup from the

Father's hands. That cup, drunk to the dregs, opened the way for the Holy Spirit.

And here: "Likewise the Spirit helps us in our weakness; for we do not know how to pray as we ought, but that very Spirit intercedes with sighs too deep for words. And God, who searches the heart, knows what is the mind of the Spirit" (Rom 8:26–27).

"In hope we were saved" (cf. Rom 8:24).

10. Speaking at the Areopagus, the apostle said of the "unknown God" that "in him we live and move and have our being" (cf. Acts 17:23, 28).

In him who is the Unity of Father, Son, and Holy Spirit.

In him we live, we move, and we exist. This is confirmed by *prayer*, which first states that we *"live and move and have our being"* in God because *"we too are his offspring."*

NOTES

"*Credo . . .*" is from the hymn *Adoro te devote.*

CURATOR'S NOTES
BY MARTA BURGHARDT

The passage from the Acts of the Apostles (17:16–34) in which St. Paul proclaims the truth about Christ, his resurrection from the dead, and his ascension into heaven is commonly called the discourse at the Areopagus. Paul of Tarsus was not one of the twelve apostles, nor did he belong to the larger group of Jesus' disciples, but he was a Pharisee and persecuted Christians. After his conversion, he became the apostle to the Gentiles. This apostolic ministry brought him from his native Cilicia (now Turkey), through Macedonia, to Greece. Paul, arriving for the first time in Athens, even though he was not a stranger to Hellenic culture, was troubled at the sight of the city full of idols, above all because he had been educated in the spirit of a monotheistic religion. His discourse at the foot of the Acropolis, in the square known as the *agora* where the political and intellectual life of Athens came together, drew the attention of the Stoics, the Epicureans, and many foreigners, who suggested that he offer his teachings from the height of the Areopagus. Here St. Paul made his historic speech.

Karol Wojtyła took the speech of St. Paul and made it the starting point for a cycle of thirteen catecheses. We do not know to whom these catecheses were addressed, when or if they were delivered, or whether they were ever made public. The fact is that they are preserved in the form of a manuscript composed of thirty-nine sheets (28 x 22 cm in size), written on both sides in black ink, in beautiful handwriting, but with corrections. All the pages contain the numbering made by the author, from number 1 to 78. At the top left corner of each page appears the inscription "AMDG" (*Ad Maiorem Dei Gloriam*): "For the greater glory of God"; or "J + M": "Jesus and Mary"; or the monogram composed of the Greek letters *chi* and *rho*, which stands for "Christ" (from the Greek Χριϲτοϲ). Latin verses are written at the top right corner of every page. The first pages offer lines taken from the treatise of St. Louis-Marie Grignion de Montfort: "*Totus Tuus ego sum et omnia mea Tua sunt. Accipio Te in mea omnia. Praebe mihi cor Tuum, Maria*": "I am totally yours and all that is mine is yours. I offer you in everything that is mine. Give me your heart, Mary." Along the tops of the following pages appear the verses that form the stanzas of the Gospel Sequence *Victimae paschali laudes*: "Christians, to the Paschal Victim, Offer your thankful praises . . . ," which is proclaimed on Easter Sunday and during the Easter octave. Following that is the Gospel Sequence *Veni, Sancte Spiritus*: "Come, Holy Spirit," which is part of the liturgy of the Solemnity of Pentecost; then, the eucharistic hymn attributed to St. Thomas Aquinas, *Adoro te devote*: "I devoutly adore you, hidden God."[1]

The handwritten texts of the meditations were subsequently typed by another person, which seems plausible due to the presence of some mistakes in the typewritten version. In the seventy-two pages of the typewritten version, the verses of the prayers and sequences do not appear at the top; many biblical quotations have been added to provide the missing citations of chapters and verses, and others have been corrected and arranged according to the text of the Holy Bible. This shows that Wojtyła wrote the biblical quotations by heart; otherwise he would have written them exactly, inserting the numbers of verses. It can also be assumed that Wojtyła knew almost from memory the conciliar writings from which he quotes several passages. The same is true for the quotations of the Latin hymns placed in the upper right of each page of the handwritten manuscript. It should be emphasized that the typewritten version does not contain any trace of modifications by Wojtyła, nor additions or clarifications, so it is not possible to know whether he ever returned to this text.

The handwritten text was used as the basis for the original Polish language edition; that edition provided footnotes that noted the deletions made by the author in the manuscript and the variants of the typewritten version (mistakes were omitted).[2] Several deleted words and phrases in the handwritten text have not been eliminated completely; some, in fact, refer to some other part of the text. Wojtyła also introduced additions to the handwritten text, but due to lack of space, he placed them in the side margin of the sheet or at the bottom of the page, marking them with the symbols "F" and "x."

We can deduce that these catecheses were written in 1965, or just afterward, because they contain references to the Second Vatican Council, its *Declaration on the Relation of the Church to Non-Christian Religions, Nostra Aetate* (approved October 28, 1965), the *Dogmatic Constitution on Divine Revelation, Dei Verbum* (approved November 18, 1965), and the *Pastoral Constitution on the Church in the Modern World, Gaudium et Spes* (approved December 7, 1965).

The aforementioned date of writing (or an immediately later one) is confirmed by the fact that the biblical quotations, also in the typewritten version, are taken from the *Millennium Bible*, published for the first time in Poland in 1965. The presence of references to the philosophy of Plato and Aristotle, Thomism, phenomenology, the writings of St. Augustine of Hippo, figures of late-ancient Christian thought, and the Greek poets all may suggest that these texts were written for intellectual circles, perhaps academic; however, Archbishop Wojtyła does not define the texts as lectures, but as catecheses or reflections. Unfortunately, no information has been preserved to indicate whether this cycle of catechesis was presented over thirteen consecutive days or thirteen consecutive weeks (that is, about three months). From the text itself we cannot even deduce who the audience is intended to be, because the author addresses "all those who are listening to me" or "the people of our time." We must also take into account the fact that in 1966, the year of the Millennium was celebrated in the Polish Church, that is, the one thousandth anniversary of the "Christianization" of Poland, or of its "baptism" and the constitution of the Polish state; consequently, the commitments of the Archbishop of Kraków were particularly intense. Therefore it is possible that this conciliar father wrote the cycle of catechesis in Rome. As we read in his letter of November 15, 1965, to Wanda Półtawska from the Eternal City, "There is much time to reflect here. The space of prayer is well organized and included in the program, and there is enough free time, which is rare in Kraków. There is also the possibility of getting out and going somewhere on Saturday or Sunday—and in Italy there is always something interesting to see." The Metropolitan of Kraków, during his stay in Rome, certainly had the opportunity to visit the places known to him since youth, from the time of his university studies, and linked to the Apostle to the Gentiles, such as the Mamertine Prison; the Abbey of the Tre Fontane, which, according to tradition, is the place of the martyrdom of St. Paul; and the Basilica of St. Paul outside the Walls, where the saint is buried. The hypothesis that the cycle of catechesis was composed in Rome is also supported by the paper used, on which we see the watermark "*Fine Post Effe.*" It should be noted that none of the poetic, philosophical, or theological works preserved in the archives of the Metropolitan Curia of Kraków were written on sheets of paper of this type. Another argument supporting this thesis is the fact that the author seems to have thought of an Italian translation, because at the end of the fourth

catechesis, in the typewritten version, the following anno-
tation appears, which does not appear in the handwritten
text: "For the Italian translation: '*l'amor di sé fino all'indifferenza per Iddio [...] l'amore a Dio fino all'indifferenza per
sé*' (S. Augustinus, *De civitate Dei*, 14, 28: CSEL 40, 2, 56)."

It seems that the Latin quotation was probably written
from memory, due to the fact that in the handwritten text
Archbishop Wojtyła left an empty parenthesis close to it,
obviously with the intention of completing it at a later time;
the bibliographic reference to the Latin version appears
in the typewritten version. We cannot say with certainty
whether the catecheses were written for Italian listeners or
readers, but we can say with absolute conviction that they
are universal and timeless.

As we have already noted, Archbishop Wojtyła's manuscript contains many references to the Declaration *Nostra
Aetate*. It addresses the religions of Judaism, Buddhism,
and Hinduism. We know that in the spirit of the provisions
of the council, the Archbishop of Kraków was very active
in interreligious dialogue. To cite a few examples: at the
invitation of the archbishop, the rector of the Orthodox
parish at Szpitalna Street in Kraków regularly attended the
meetings of the Catholic Intelligentsia Club held on Sienna
Street; in November 1969, Karol Wojtyła met with Wanda
Dynowska Umadevi, a woman who collaborated with the
Dalai Lama and was committed to helping Tibetan refu-
gees, especially children; in February 1969, Wojtyła visited two synagogues in the Jewish section of Kazimierz in

Kraków, demonstrating his openness to dialogue with the Jews. Many more examples of this kind of activity could be listed.

Two millennia after the footsteps of the Apostle to the Gentiles, John Paul II went to Athens in May 2001. He was nearly at the end of his life. He stayed on Greek soil for only twenty-four hours but achieved in that brief time more than his predecessors over the centuries. On May 4, John Paul II and Christodoulos, the Archbishop of Athens and Primate of the Orthodox Church of Greece, signed a joint declaration on the Christian roots of Europe. Although circumstances did not allow Peter's successor to ascend the Areopagus, the words of the apostle Paul resounded again with great force: "Now I appeal to you, brothers and sisters, by the name of our Lord Jesus Christ, that all of you be in agreement and that there be no divisions among you, but that you be united in the same mind and the same purpose" (1 Cor 1:10).

From Greece the Holy Father then went on to Syria. He was the first pope in history to enter a mosque: in Damascus, on May 6, 2001, he visited the Umayyad Mosque. In his speeches on that occasion, he emphasized above all the common points of the two religions, Christianity and Islam, emphasizing that dialogue between Christians and Muslims must be illuminated by mutual forgiveness.

The words of the apostle Paul spoken in the Athenian Areopagus always had a profound significance for Archbishop Wojtyła. They did not lose value for him once he became pope; this is demonstrated by the fact that he frequently referred to that Pauline discourse. They retained their significance for Wojtyła as a poet; in his *Roman Triptych*, a poem he wrote in 2003, in the second part, "Meditations on the Book of Genesis at the Threshold of the Sistine Chapel," he takes up the words of the Apostle to the Gentiles:

> "In him we live and move and have our being" —
> says Paul to the Areopagus of Athens —
> Who is He?
> He is like an ineffable space embracing all things.
> He is the Creator:
> He embraces all, summoning to existence from
> nothing,
> not only in the beginning but continually.
> Everything endures, is constantly becoming.[3]

NOTES

1. These lines were written sequentially at the top of each handwritten manuscript page. They are a devotional exercise of the author and do not correspond to the content of the pages on which they are written.

2. This edition integrates the handwritten version with the additions and specifications of the typewritten one, omitting the notes containing the list of deletions made by the author in the manuscript; uprooted from the Polish linguistic context and transferred to another language, they would be incomprehensible and meaningless.

3. John Paul II, *The Poetry of John Paul II: Roman Triptych: Meditations*, trans. Jerzy Peterkiewicz (Washington, DC: United States Conference of Catholic Bishops, 2003), 13.

George Weigel is a Catholic author, theologian, and distinguished senior fellow and the William E. Simon Chair in Catholic Studies at the Ethics and Public Policy Center.

Scott Hahn is a popular Catholic theologian, author, speaker, and apologist who founded the Saint Paul Center for Biblical Theology and teaches at Franciscan University of Steubenville.

Marta Burghardt is the author of *An Unknown Friend of Karol Wojtyła: Wincenty Bałys* and is the Italian translator of *Young Poems by Karol Wojtyła*.

AVE

AVE MARIA PRESS

Founded in 1865, Ave Maria Press,
a ministry of the Congregation of
Holy Cross, is a Catholic publishing
company that serves the spiritual and
formative needs of the Church and its
schools, institutions, and ministers;
Christian individuals and families; and
others seeking spiritual nourishment.

———

For a complete listing of titles from

Ave Maria Press

Sorin Books

Forest of Peace

Christian Classics

visit avemariapress.com